The Response to Intervention Handbook

The Response to Intervention Handbook

Moving from Theory to Practice

Andrea Ogonosky

Park Place Publications

Austin, Texas

1601 Rio Grande, Suite 441

Austin, Texas 78701

(512) 478-2113 • Fax: (512) 495-9955

www.parkplacepubs.com

First Printing: February 2008
Second Printing: April 2008
Third Printing: May 2008
Fourth Printing: October 2008
Fifth Printing: May 2009

ISBN 978-1-60585-184-6

To James, Kimberly, and Emily,
whose unbelievable support of my career
has allowed me to pursue my passion—
enriching the lives of children

Contents

Acknowledgments

I would like to acknowledge some of the people who have supported my efforts in this endeavor. Without their support and encouragement this project would not have been successful. Thanks to Carolyn Baird and Willis ISD administration for their willingness to provide their RtI forms as samples for this book. I learn daily from the outstanding professionals in Willis ISD. Dr. Gail Cheramie and Dr. Carol Booth were instrumental in providing feedback, examples, and expertise in RtI. The thoughtful insights offered by Mary Kay Allbright and Laura Abbott of Conroe ISD as I struggled at times to define RtI in practical terms for the readers of this book were much appreciated. I also thank my editor and new friend, Rosemary Wetherold, for her excellent dedication and technical expertise. And, finally, this project would not have been completed without the endless hours of "alone time" my family unselfishly gave me.

Illustrations

Figures

Tables

Forms and Checklists

Introduction

The educational approach known as Response to Intervention, or RtI, began to gain momentum in 2001, when the Learning Disabilities Summit, sponsored by the U.S. Department of Education, endorsed its use for identifying learning disabilities. This endorsement—along with the subsequent passage of both the No Child Left Behind Act of 2001 (NCLB) and the Individuals with Disabilities Education Improvement Act of 2004 (IDEA)—propelled RtI onto a national level in the field of education.

The goal of RtI is to improve academic outcomes for all students by intervening early when any student shows signs that he or she is struggling. Data are gathered so that instruction is matched to the individual student and so that research-based interventions focus on the unique needs of the struggling learner. The student's progress—that is, his or her response to the interventions—is monitored and is used in making decisions about strategies for the student's success.

My motivation for writing this book arose during my consulting work with school districts as I watched administrators struggle to put the theory of RtI into practice. The purpose of this book is twofold. First, it will help administrators and school staff use their existing district- and campus-level support systems to implement RtI in a seamless three-tier process that is both time- and cost-efficient. Second, this guide will help parents and educational specialists understand the RtI process and their roles in it.

As I have worked with campus administrators, staff, and parents, I have seen extraordinary successes with RtI. I have witnessed growth in teacher confidence and skills due to increased staff development opportunities, and growth in student motivation that is directly tied to self-monitoring and awareness of the slightest skill development. For example, one second-grader demonstrated his ability to use collected data to come up with additional interventions that led to continued gains in his reading fluency. He also asked the RtI team for tutoring from a high school buddy when his mother began working at night and could not read with him on a daily basis as planned.

The chapters that follow describe Response to Intervention in detail and provide a step-by-step guide to its implementation. Chapter 1 introduces the theory behind the process, and the underlying philosophy regarding data-based decision making. Chapter 2 is a guide to laying the foundations for implementing RtI successfully. Chapter 3 defines the first tier of RtI in practical terms, focusing on the importance of universal data collection and interventions. The journey into the RtI process continues in Chapter 4, which defines the second tier of support and data collection. Chapter 5 covers the most intensive phase of RtI and offers insight for developing the necessary supports for successful problem solving and outcomes.

RtI involves assessment and both academic and behavioral interventions, and each of these aspects of RtI is carried out in a three-tier flow. The unified RtI process can be envisioned as three sides of a tetrahedron:

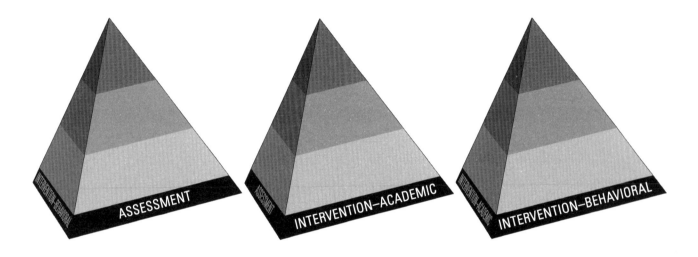

These illustrations are used throughout the book, with the RtI aspect and tier under discussion highlighted so that their place in the unified RtI process can be comprehended in a glance.

Embedded in the chapters are "Lessons Learned" sections to help connect the theory presented to real-life examples of successes (and missteps to avoid) during RtI implementation. These lessons are based on my experiences from consulting in school districts in Texas, Arkansas, and Pennsylvania. All of these districts and their campuses are learning daily, just as yours will be. Some of these lessons are more challenging than others, but I encourage you to regard them all as guides for your own growth and success with RtI.

A wide variety of useful checklists and forms appear throughout the book. These documents are meant to be examples of how to integrate information and develop parameters for transitioning into RtI, as well as to emphasize the importance of data collection. The readiness survey and accompanying team action plan were developed during consultations with districts as it became evident that many administrators needed a guide through the process. The documents related to fidelity are offered to support the value of consistent implementation of RtI.

Blank versions of all of these forms and checklists are included on an accompanying CD as both Microsoft® Word documents and Adobe® Acrobat® PDFs. The CD also contains checklists and worksheets (organized by RtI tier) for district-wide planning of assessments and interventions; criteria for scientific-based research; and observation of instructional strategies. Although these documents are copyrighted, the copyright is waived for educational support use by purchasers of this book.

Appendix A contains answers to a range of questions I am often asked when consulting with school districts about RtI. Sample forms that one Texas district developed to suit its needs are included in Appendix B; and Appendix C is a handy list of online resources that are most helpful in guiding a district as it develops and implements its own RtI process. At the back of the book are a glossary of terms related to the RtI process, as well as abbreviations that have been used in the text, plus a bibliography of useful references.

RtI is an exciting process, but it requires patience, persistence, and vision. The expectations and attitudes that administrators bring to the campus will set the tone for change. Dream big, and you'll see changes that go from the ordinary to the extraordinary.

Chapter 1

What Is "Response to Intervention"?

Response to Intervention (RtI) is not really a new process. Many districts have implemented parts of this system for the past several years. However, in RtI there is a major shift in responsibility for struggling learners—from special education to the general education classroom. View RtI as a seamless problem-solving process that enhances the learning of *all* children by using consultation and support among *all* educators—combining the unique talents of both general educators and specialists. With RtI, high-quality instruction is matched to student needs by using frequent data collection to guide all decisions regarding student progress.

This process should look very familiar to teachers because they already use this approach informally on a regular basis. RtI simply formalizes this problem-solving method. When educators shift their mind-set and come to view all professionals on campus—general and special educators alike—as available for consultation and support for all children, great things can happen. Teachers begin to feel empowered to tap into resources they previously believed were available only if the student had been given a "label" for services; parents become active partners in intervention support; and students take ownership of their learning.

Core Characteristics of RtI

The core characteristics of the RtI model have been described by the National Association of State Directors of Special Education (NASDSE 2005) and can be summarized as follows:

- **All children can be taught** using high-quality instruction in the general education setting. This belief is communicated daily in schools across America with the slogan commonly displayed on doors and windows: "All children can learn."
- **Intervention occurs early,** when learning and behavior problems are small. It is far easier (and more effective) to intervene using **universal,**

researched-based strategies when a problem is first developing than to wait until larger deficits require more intense forms of intervention.

- To meet the instructional and behavioral needs of students, applying graduated levels of interventions, or **tiers of interventions,** is crucial. **Tier 1** applies to all students, and **Tiers 2 and 3** apply to students who need greater levels of intervention. The multi-tier approach helps campus support teams tailor their instruction and services to struggling learners.

- Within the multi-tier model, the **problem-solving method** has been highly effective in helping to clearly define student needs and to match those needs to instructional strategies and interventions. Using this method for making decisions includes asking a hierarchy of questions whose answers are driven by data:

  1. Is there a problem? If so, what is it, and why is it happening?
  2. How can we use the curriculum to solve the problem?
  3. What interventions can we use to solve the problem? How can we implement them?
  4. Did the interventions work? Or do we need to try something else?

In RtI, this problem-solving approach is applied to *all* students within *all* tiers.

- **Interventions and curricula are based on research** and are scientifically validated, as required by NCLB and IDEA.

- **Student progress is monitored** by frequently collecting data to determine the effectiveness of interventions that have been implemented. The data are directly related to the curriculum that has been introduced, and they are sensitive to the slightest skill development.

- **All decisions are data-based.** This is a critical feature and the one that is probably the most difficult to implement with **fidelity.** This feature requires that all systems for ongoing assessment be in place.

- Decisions are driven by all of the data gathered from **assessment** within each tier. Assessment tools are used for the **screening of all students (Tier 1)** to determine which ones are not making the same academic and behavioral gains as their peers; for **diagnostics (Tiers 1 and 2)** to determine which students are unable to demonstrate essential academic and behavioral skills; and for **progress monitoring (Tiers 2 and 3)** to guide decision making about interventions.

---

research-based strategies Instructional designs and recommendations that have been demonstrated through formal scientific research to improve learning.

tiers of interventions Levels of increasingly intense interventions to help students learn.

problem-solving method A set of specific steps for solving problems related to the challenging aspects of teaching and learning.

curriculum The set of courses, coursework, and content offered at school.

fidelity The degree to which something is carried out as designed, intended, or planned.

assessment The process of using evaluation tools to gather and analyze information about student skill level and progress and the effectiveness of curricula and teaching methods.

screening A type of assessment used to predict which students are likely to experience difficulty learning.

diagnostics A more precise form of assessment that analyzes individual student strengths and weaknesses.

progress monitoring Frequent measurement of student progress in a brief, repeatable, reliable, and scientifically valid way; usually performed at predetermined intervals to allow for timely modification of instructional design to suit the student's needs.

A Three-Tier Approach

instruction The act of delivering information so that learning can occur.

learning rate The pace of a student's skill acquisition; one of the elements used for making decisions in RtI.

performance Measurable outcomes that are characteristic of student learning.

eligibility conditions Conditions defined by federal and state governments for determining whether children qualify for receiving special education services.

RtI focuses on delivering high-quality instruction and interventions based on data that document learning rates and levels of performance. These data guide the RtI team in making important decisions about the intensity and duration of interventions for individual students. The core components of RtI are multiple tiers of interventions; high-quality instruction based on scientific research; data-based decision making; and research-based interventions.

Much has already been written about the current "wait-to-fail" model that prompted the President's Commission on Excellence in Education and IDEA to promote early intervention. In RtI, district resources are arranged to provide a unified system of education that incorporates early intervention. To accomplish this process in your district, your general education and special education systems must be unified.

The starting place is to recognize several important characteristics of RtI. First, RtI is not a special education initiative, although most district personnel have been interpreting it that way. Additionally, under RtI, a child does not need an eligibility condition, or "label," to receive individualized support. And finally, procedural guidelines to frame the process and guide continuous improvement must be in place at both the district and campus levels.

RtI emphasizes assessment as the foundation for making decisions and for monitoring instructional effectiveness. This assessment provides the data for structured problem solving. Within that decision-making process, team members must be flexible as they identify which resources are already available and which additional resources are needed to support learning.

There are many variations of the tiered model of RtI. The three major components of this approach are often described in words (table 1.1) and can also be conceptualized visually, with the major components forming three sides of a tiered tetrahedron (figures 1.1–1.3; details presented in these figures and in table 1.1 are discussed in depth in Chapters 3–5). Often the three-tier model indicates increasingly intense levels of intervention, applied to decreasing numbers of students (table 1.2 and figure 1.4). All students receive Tier 1 interventions, regardless of any other tiers of intervention that may be occurring for individual students. Likewise, students who move from Tier 2 to Tier 3 will receive intensified Tier 2 interventions. Some districts have proposed a fourth tier in their model; in that case, Tier 3 remains within the regular education domain, and Tier 4 indicates a formal referral to special education. In this book, as in most tiered RtI models, special education is encompassed in Tier 3.

Table 1.1. Elements of a three-tier RtI approach

RtI Components by Tier	Description	Procedures for Implementation
TIER 1 • Universal screening • Diagnostics • Progress monitoring *High-quality instructional and behavioral supports are provided for all students in general education.*	• Collection and sharing of benchmark data among teachers, principals, district staff, and parents (data are collected in fall, winter, and spring) • Specific, objective measures of problem areas, not anecdotal information or opinions	• School personnel conduct universal screening of academic and behavioral skills. • Teachers implement a variety of research-supported instructional strategies. • Ongoing curriculum-based assessment (continuous progress monitoring) is used to guide high-quality instruction. • Students receive differentiated instruction based on data from ongoing assessments.
TIER 2 • Baseline data collection • Diagnostics • Progress monitoring • Written plan of accountability • Comparison of pre- and post–intervention data *Students whose performance and rate of progress lag behind those of peers in their classroom, school, or district receive more-specialized prevention or remediation within general education.*	• Curriculum-based measurement (CBM) to determine whether a problem area is an issue with the student or the core curriculum • Which interventions will be tried that are different? Who will do them? When? Where? For how long? • Frequent collection of a variety of data to examine student performance over time and evaluate interventions in order to make data-based decisions • Data-based decision making for intervention effectiveness	• Curriculum-based measures are used to identify which students continue to need assistance with specific kinds of skills. • Collaborative problem solving is used to design and implement instructional support for students that may consist of more-individualized strategies and interventions. • Student progress is monitored frequently to determine intervention effectiveness. • Systematic assessment is conducted to determine the fidelity with which instruction and interventions are implemented. • Parents are informed and are involved in planning. • General education teachers receive support (training, consultation, direct services).
TIER 3 • Increased intensity of interventions *Tier 3 includes all the elements of Tier 2. The difference between Tier 2 and Tier 3 is the frequency and group size of the intervention treatment.*	• The most intensive phase of RtI • Fidelity of intervention ensured by documentation • If progress monitoring does not establish improvement after intervention phase is implemented, referral for multidisciplinary assessment for special education is warranted.	• Procedures are consistent with those of Tier 2. • Intensity of interventions increases; treatment time and group size vary with intervention.

Source: Adapted from a chart developed by Andrea Ogonosky, Gail Cheramie, and Carol Booth, 2006.

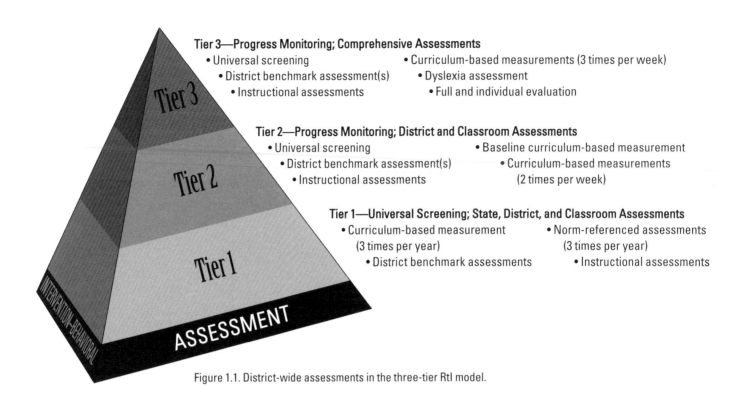

Figure 1.1. District-wide assessments in the three-tier RtI model.

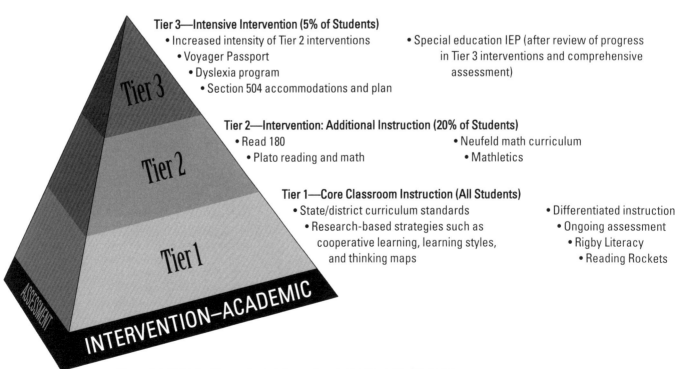

Figure 1.2. District-wide academic interventions in the three-tier RtI model.

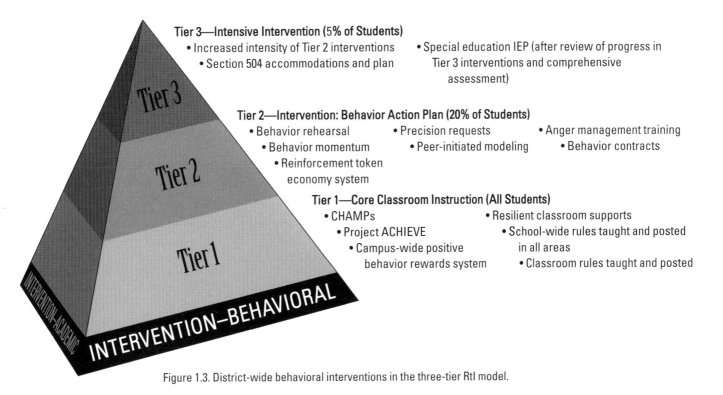

Figure 1.3. District-wide behavioral interventions in the three-tier RtI model.

Data-Based Problem Solving

Problem solving in RtI is completely data driven. This is a big shift in thinking for staff. Teachers routinely collect data in the form of observations, criterion-referenced testing, and student products. The dramatic shift happens during the problem-solving process. Typically, staff tend to make decisions based on emotions and not on collected data. RtI data collection focuses on student learning rates, which can then be directly linked to intervention effectiveness (thus removing the subjective factor).

criterion-referenced assessment A measure of performance in terms of a clearly defined learning task.

student product Something created by a student to demonstrate learning of a skill.

Table 1.2. Levels of intervention and assessment in the three-tier RtI model

Tier 1 (100% of students)	Tier 2 (about 20% of students)	Tier 3 (about 5% of students)
• High-quality instruction and behavioral supports for all students • Decision making based on universal screening and benchmarking *Approximately 80% of students receive only Tier 1 interventions and assessments. The remaining students will also receive Tier 2, and some of those will also receive Tier 3.*	• Targeted interventions • Progress monitoring (CBM) to inform decisions *Approximately 15% of students receive only Tier 1 and Tier 2 interventions and assessments. The remaining 5% will also receive Tier 3.*	• Increased intensity of targeted interventions • Continued progress monitoring • Possible referral to special education

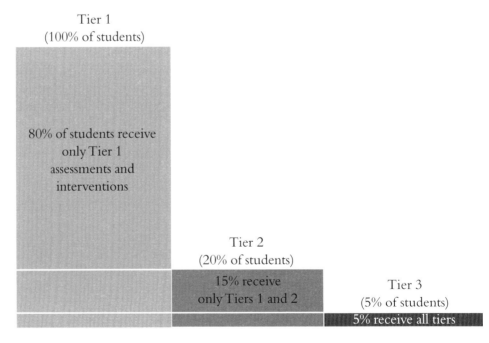

Figure 1.4. Approximate percentages of students receiving each tier of assessments and interventions. All students receive Tier 1 assessments and interventions. A portion of students also receive Tier 2 assessments and interventions, and a small percentage receive all three tiers.

Lessons Learned: One campus was struggling with low staff morale, poor student motivation, and a perceived lack of opportunities to provide interventions to children. Year 1 data collection (pre–RtI) revealed that on this particular campus 75 children were referred for special education testing for learning disabilities. Of the 75 students referred, only 24 were found to have a learning disability. The remaining 51 children received no additional interventions—the assessment *was* the intervention. This was a very poor process, because the children who received no additional interventions had fallen further behind by the time the assessment process was completed.

Compare this outcome with that of year 3 of RtI on the same campus: 24 children who were found to need Tier 3 interventions subsequently met eligibility criteria for special education as students with learning disabilities. The more important number, however, is the 116 children who received individualized interventions within Tiers 2 and 3 (not special education) and demonstrated increased learning rates within their areas of difficulty.

The rewards for using a systematic problem-solving process are that resources for students are used more flexibly; parents become more involved; interventions are implemented within the general education setting, with supports from additional staff (school psychologists, speech and language pathologists, physical therapists, social workers); and student achievement increases.

Chapter 2

Getting Ready to Implement RtI

Establishing Response to Intervention in your school system will require significant changes, beginning with the primary roles and responsibilities of all staff and of parents. Campus administrators must embrace the philosophy of RtI before attempting to carry out the process. Along with promoting change, leadership in the transition becomes a key element in the success of implementation.

Promoting a Shift in Philosophy

In his book *Failing Forward: Turning Mistakes into Stepping Stones for Success,* John C. Maxwell (2000) identified four factors to promote success when leading an organization through change. To achieve success in implementing RtI, the administrator must first focus on the **relationships** that have been developed with staff and parents. These relationships will affect every aspect of decision making along the way. The next factor is to have **big dreams;** all effective leaders can achieve a vision with the right team. How high the team will soar depends on the **attitude** the leader brings to the change process. Lastly, every outcome will be the result of the personal **leadership skills** the administrator possesses. Therefore, continued personal and professional growth should be non-negotiable, particularly when it comes to understanding and committing to the concepts of RtI. The most effective leaders of RtI have embraced change and observed the incredible positive aspects of supporting all students and meeting their needs, not with a labeling system, but through a seamless process that acknowledges all types of learners.

Change can be very difficult. What is most important in helping school staff and parents move toward RtI is to provide the necessary supports that will enable personal growth and to increase trust that those supports will continue to be available. From the start, all administrators must actively and publicly support the RtI process.

According to Sylvia Méndez-Morse (1992), effective leaders of change have some characteristics in common. Leadership begins with a vision that is developed and shared. The leaders in education who have been able to accomplish great changes are those who were proactive and took risks. They were able to recognize the evolving needs of the staff and parents, to anticipate necessary changes, and to effectively challenge the notion of "status quo." Additionally, an administrator's abilities both to communicate and to listen influence the shift in philosophy significantly.

Several barriers will present themselves at this time of change. For example, campus leaders will need to identify which interventions currently being used on the campus are effective for struggling learners. They must then analyze those interventions; decide whether the interventions are research-based, as defined by the No Child Left Behind Act and the Individuals with Disabilities Education Improvement Act; and set the expectation that all personnel will implement the interventions with fidelity. As administrators begin this inventory and evaluation, they will face barriers from those who are resisting the change or are having difficulty understanding it. Commonly, statements such as these are heard during an initial meeting about RtI: "I have so many students in my class that I cannot possibly do this"; "Where is special education? This is really their issue"; and "I have tried everything I know. This cannot be a problem with the curriculum or instruction—it surely must be a problem with the child." One of the biggest challenges for all administrators is to bring their educators to understand that RtI is not merely a referral process to special education but, rather, is a process that focuses on high-quality instructional practices and research-based interventions to support the struggling learner. RtI is not a vehicle on the road to special education—it is a journey of interventions to support learning.

Lessons Learned: Understanding that the change process will take time is extremely important. Implementing RtI does not happen overnight—it will take several years to develop. Patience and flexibility are the keys to success.

Laying the Groundwork for Change

A major concern in the public school system is to help struggling learners progress in the curriculum. Parents and staff can become very frustrated when a child falls behind in learning to read, write, or do math. Response to Intervention is essential to making accurate decisions about the effectiveness of general and remedial instruction. RtI promotes the understanding that how well a subject is taught gauges how well the children will learn. In the purest form, RtI is simply about personalizing information for individual students to promote their academic success. The intent of the process is to decrease the number of "curriculum casualties" by ensuring that all students are given high-quality instruction with fidelity. It is an opportunity for educators to resolve students' learning difficulties by primarily focusing on student needs and not on special education eligibility decisions. RtI is about *what* will be done rather than *where* it will be done, and *how* to intervene as opposed to *who* will do the intervention.

Once district administrators have made the commitment to move forward, the campus administrator needs to inventory all available assessment methods and resources that are important for implementing RtI. Information gathered will focus on the specific needs for each student within each tier of the process. The following steps need to be taken during the transition to RtI:

1. Inventory existing assessment structure: current district benchmarks, state-mandated testing, assessments to identify students who may need specialized programs, and teacher data collection (student products, district-required standardized assessments, pre-referral assessments, special education assessment practices). ***District and campus level***

2. Check for alignment of assessment tools with curriculum. Which of the current assessments measure whether the student is learning what is expected? ***District and campus level***

3. Select universal screening measures and choose dates of administration (3 times per year, in the fall, winter, and spring). ***District level (to ensure consistency across campuses)***

4. Design a user-friendly database for results from universal screening. ***District level***

5. Develop guidelines for decision making. Review existing district forms and modify them to conform to the RtI process. ***District level***

Once administrators and staff understand the scope of the change in intervening with struggling learners—particularly the way in which the campuses will now evaluate individual student progress—then district *and* campus administrators must work together to create a solid foundation of readiness for implementing RtI. The district should develop comprehensive guidelines for implementation, including how current campus assessment tools will be inventoried and how existing pre-referral and intervention practices will be evaluated. At this stage, administrators need to focus on campus leadership (knowledge and skills), existing intervention teams, core curriculum, current screening procedures, and needs for professional development. To fully embrace the RtI process, the school district must expand its comprehensive plans to incorporate an assessment of readiness and campus foundational strengths (administrator attitude, available resources, etc.) for putting RtI into practice. The forms on pages 25–29 (the RtI District Fidelity Checklist, Action Plan Readiness Survey, Team Action Plan, Campus Fidelity Checklist, and Action Plan Checklist for Campus Administra-

standardized assessment A type of test that is developed according to standard procedures and is administered and scored in a consistent manner for all students.

pre-referral assessment An evaluation of whether further assessment is needed to determine a student's special education eligibility. This type of assessment does not focus on developing intervention strategies.

tor) may be useful at this stage. For a discussion of the importance of the fidelity of RtI implementation within the district, campus, and classroom, see Chapter 3.

It Is Time to Begin

It would be wise to begin the entire process of introducing RtI by having several planning meetings (at least 6 to 8) at the district administrative level. Attendees should include the superintendent and assistant superintendent(s), curriculum coordinators (elementary and secondary), special education administrators, reading and math intervention coordinators, the pre-referral coordinator, the counseling coordinator, and parent liaisons.

The agenda of the first two meetings should focus on training the attendees in understanding the model of RtI, what NCLB and IDEA mean when they refer to research-based instructional practices and interventions, and the roles of general education staff, special education staff, and parent involvement. Plan to use at least two of the remaining meetings to discuss the change process and how to align current practices with RtI.

Once the group demonstrates not only an *understanding* but a *willingness* to move forward, the real planning can begin. Be prepared for initial frustrations and barriers that will surface, as all involved at this level must first shift their own philosophies regarding curriculum, teaching, and intervention. At this level, the main issues to surface initially are related to turfs. Curriculum specialists may become defensive during discussions on evaluating current practices and aligning them with NCLB standards for research-based strategies. Special education personnel may focus on eligibility issues. Reading specialists may hone in on resources.

It is during the initial planning meetings that persons in authority must be willing to accept modifications of current practices. All personnel on the RtI planning team will invest time and effort in designing and implementing new systems for working with all students. The districts that have been most successful were able to move beyond this initial resistance, which can be very large. It is most important to honor all perspectives and not become defensive and entrenched in thinking, "This is how we have always done it."

If there is resistance, it is best to resolve it during these initial meetings at the district administrative level, because the decisions made then will form the perspective that ultimately influences the campus leadership. Stop and take the time to investigate research-based options and to address all concerns at this stage. Although this can be uncomfortable, the benefits of not rushing through this particular stage are significant.

Once the initial district leadership team is in agreement on the philosophy and district perspective on RtI, several important tasks must be addressed. This team must prepare guidance for the development of RtI in the district:

1. Discuss how to provide needed staff development. Create a staff development plan that includes training and materials.
    a. RtI process
    b. NCLB and IDEA regulations
    c. Curriculum alignment with progress monitoring (curriculum-based measurement, or CBM—see the RtI Curriculum-Based Measurement Questions form on page 30 and the discussion of CBM in Chapter 4)
    d. Leadership training for all campus administrators

2. Generate district models of assessments, research-based academic interventions, and research-based behavioral interventions (refer to figures 1.1–1.3 as examples).
    a. Arrange assessments in three tiers.
    b. Align academic and behavioral interventions with the appropriate tiers, according to intervention intensity.
    c. Ensure that the assessment tools and interventions identified are available to the RtI team and school staff.

3. Select members of the campus-based team. (Assign one core RtI team per campus; two teams may be necessary on secondary campuses or very large campuses.)
    a. Train administrators on appropriate membership and roles.
    b. Plan and support selection of the campus team.
    c. Train the team.
        i. Procedural guidelines
        ii. Problem-solving process
        iii. Core curriculum standards and assessment of standards
        iv. Tiers of assessment
        v. Tiers of intervention
        vi. Collaboration and critical skill development

4. Establish guidelines for the campus team process.
    a. Generate norms of meetings, including regularly scheduled times (campus consultations or individual student meetings).
    b. Decide how parents will be included in the process.
    c. Create a system for collection, analysis, and publication of data.
    d. Determine decision points for moving students between tiers.
    e. Practice team roles and meeting procedures before implementing RtI.
        i. Identify how data will be examined and discussed.
        ii. Prioritize gaps in student achievement and behavioral issues.
        iii. Establish an action plan with measurable outcomes and data collection.

5. Set up a system for faculty, staff, and parents to communicate with each other about the RtI process.

curriculum-based measurement Any set of assessment procedures that use direct observation and recording of a student's performance in a local curriculum to gather information for making instructional decisions.

decision points Guidelines developed by the district for gauging whether a student may need more intensive interventions within the RtI process.

> **Lessons Learned:** In my consultations with several school districts, it became apparent that scheduling the district-level team meetings was most effective when they were approximately 3 hours long and occurred twice a month. Some district-level teams that met only once a month spent much of the meeting on reviewing previous decisions, which took time away from problem solving for the next stages.

Planning for Staff Development

In order for RtI to be successful, all staff must understand the district's philosophy regarding the RtI process—and the rationale behind it. According to the National Association of State Directors of Special Education (NASDSE 2005), effective staff development plans should follow standards adopted by the National Staff Development Council (2001). These standards form a strong foundation for designing, implementing, and supporting staff development regarding RtI. They focus on integrating staff development with school improvement data; providing assistance for administrators as they transition from the existing referral process to the supportive RtI process; and evaluating the success of the transition to RtI. For effective staff development, Showers, Joyce, and Bennett (1987) recommend that teaching modules incorporate theory, demonstration, practice, and feedback. To maintain the foundational RtI skills that the staff acquire, practice and feedback are vital, so plan for long-term training and support within the district.

Some specific modules should be incorporated in the planning for staff development. All staff should be instructed on the national and state policies driving RtI; the theory and models of RtI; use of the problem-solving process within both general education and special education; and assessment methods in all three tiers. In addition, plan for modules tailored to the needs of district and campus leaders, as well as campus staff.

The first team meetings of district leaders can cover the three-tier RtI model of assessment methods and interventions; development of training and supports for campus administrators; coordination of district resources for RtI success; and parent involvement.

For campus administrators, staff development concentrates on the following strands: RtI service delivery; allocation of staff and the budget (how to integrate resources between general and special education); leadership skills necessary for facilitating the change process; recognizing and dismantling resistance and barriers to implementation of RtI; assessing campus readiness; and planning for campus needs.

staff development
Intensive and ongoing training for teachers, administrators, and educational specialists, with a goal of improving the performance of both staff and students.

service delivery model
A description of the way in which services—such as classroom placement, strategic interventions, peer tutoring, cooperative grouping, and differentiated instruction—will be provided to students.

Staff development at the campus level emphasizes understanding the three-tier model and the district rationale for supporting RtI; research on the need for change and on evidence in support of RtI; training to develop specific skills for various research-based instructional and behavioral strategies within the general education setting (including use of district forms and other documentation; data collection techniques and interpretation of results; and decision making); and the changing roles of personnel as the RtI process is embraced on the campus.

According to NASDSE (2005), a successful staff development plan must address the critical areas of beliefs/attitudes, knowledge level, and skills. The best avenue for designing the staff development needed at each leadership level is the data collected through readiness surveys, which ascertain campus and staff needs. Opportunities for feedback throughout the year are also embedded in the staff development plan, by scheduling practice sessions and by observing the implementation of teaching strategies, interventions, and assessment.

referral-to-test model
A service delivery model in which a student must be referred to a campus team and tested for eligibility before receiving special education supports and services.

Lessons Learned: Campuses that began to pilot RtI without being given sufficient time for practice and feedback as part of staff development were not able to transition to the preventive, proactive intervention philosophy of RtI. They quickly reverted to a reactive, referral-to-test mentality (the student must have a "label" to receive a service), which slowed down RtI implementation and, in some cases, dismantled the original efforts.

Outlining Intervention Strategies

During the initial planning meetings at the district level, it is important to develop resources to guide campus administrators and staff regarding effective intervention strategies. Intervention strategies should be analyzed by the district-level personnel who are most familiar with content and behavioral areas. District-level staff may want to form small committees that will identify intervention strategies currently used within the district and determine whether they are research-based. The focus should initially center on whether current strategies are effective. Things can get very interesting when the committees begin to analyze interventions. Individual campuses may be using strategies that parents have suggested, peers have developed, or teachers have adopted based on personal experience, and these might not meet the No Child Left Behind standards for research-based curricula and interventions.

One decision the team needs to make at this stage is to adopt interventions that will be consistently implemented throughout the district. That will enable uniform planning for staff development for teachers and support personnel, as well as provide consistency when a child moves between campuses within the district. Doing this will also support one very important aspect of RtI: high-quality interventions that are implemented with fidelity and consistency. (For more on this, see "Problem Solving versus Standard Protocol" in Chapter 4.)

Lessons Learned: After inventorying the variety of programs that various campuses in the district have adopted, tread lightly when discussing their effectiveness with campus personnel. One district discovered that a very pricey program a campus had adopted to use for reading interventions did not meet standards suggested by the Florida Center for Reading Research (www.fcrr.org). When the campus administrator was contacted, he reported that the campus PTA had purchased the program. The administrator was concerned that there would be hurt feelings if the organization was told that the program did not meet the district's new standards for research-based interventions. The district-level team then developed an action plan to aid the administrator in dealing with this sensitive issue.

Establishing Guidelines for the Team Process

It is crucial that the district adopt procedural guidelines to provide the structure necessary for consistency and fidelity of the RtI process within and between campuses. These guidelines should cover the following:

- District expectations regarding the RtI process
- The operational definition of the RtI tiers
- Team membership and roles
- Team involvement on both the whole-class level and the individual student level
- Data-based problem-solving (see the RtI Implementation Guidelines for Problem Solving on page 31)
- Data-based decision points within the tiers (see the RtI Decision-Making Guide on page 32)
- Establishment of a communication system that includes parents
- Documentation forms

Documentation forms should cover communication with parents, teacher interviews, parent interviews, the team process itself, definition of outcome goals, observations of the student, fidelity of implementation, and progress monitoring.

Lessons Learned: Creating these guidelines does not have to be a cumbersome process. All districts have pre-referral teams in place. Review the district guidelines for this process, and then adjust the existing guidelines and documentation forms to conform to RtI. A great resource to guide decision making is available at Intervention Central (www.interventioncentral.org).

Selecting Campus Team Members

An essential component in building the foundation for RtI is understanding the campus RtI team process and identifying the most suitable team members. It is crucial for campus administrators to objectively evaluate current pre-referral team members and structures. The administrator's awareness of the resistance to change and potential barriers to successful RtI is vital for the appropriate selection of staff members.

The roles of the campus team are to increase support for high-quality curriculum and instruction based on data collected, to provide systematic support to teachers, to assist in aligning existing school resources for support of students and teachers, and to focus the decision-making process on data analysis. The most effective teams have a wide variety of expertise and experience across multiple areas. Core team members are supplemented by invited members as needed (table 2.1).

Table 2.1. Members of the campus RtI team

Core Members	Invited Members (as Needed)
1. Campus principal (preferred) or a designee who has decision-making authority regarding curriculum, supports, and budget issues 2. The referring teacher 3. At least one general education teacher familiar with the curriculum 4. Intervention specialist 5. Staff member knowledgeable about assessment and documentation 6. Parent of child	1. School psychologist 2. Reading/literacy specialist 3. Math specialist 4. District-level interventionists 5. Speech therapist 6. Occupational therapist 7. Counselor for struggling learners 8. Campus counselor 9. School nurse 10. Special education support/inclusion teacher

The campus RtI team engages in two distinct functions. One is to analyze the universal screening data in order to interpret trends and identify struggling learners who fall below the predetermined cutoff score. The team reviews the data to determine whether there are deficits in Tier 1 curriculum or delivery of instruction that may be contributing to students' inability to meet standards. The team uses the data in this sense to provide consultation to teachers and other staff on improving Tier 1 interventions and whole-class instruction. The second function of the team is student-centered, focusing on individual student needs. The team carries out this function after Tier 1 problem solving has been addressed and fidelity of curriculum and instruction is established. At this time, the team problem-solves to decide on individual interventions aimed at increasing the learning rate of the struggling learner.

Having staff members who are skilled in the areas of assessment and interventions is necessary, of course, but the selected team members absolutely must be motivated to participate in the RtI process. If a staff member is skilled but is not motivated or is not supportive of RtI, *do not* select this person for the team. (Such individuals are simply not ready yet, and that is okay. With time and training, they will be.) Even though a staff member may be skilled, an unsupportive attitude will poison the problem-solving process, as barriers will constantly weigh down team growth and effectiveness. On the other hand, a highly motivated staff member who has a strong positive attitude toward RtI but demonstrates skill deficits may be a very good person to select for the team, because staff development can provide the needed skills. This staff member may become an effective leader and promoter of the process, and public relations is an extremely valuable asset in the development of RtI. Other traits to look for in team members are that they are viewed as approachable and are respected by the campus staff. Team membership should be regarded as a privilege and not as "just another committee I am assigned to."

Lessons Learned: One campus administrator decided to ask a resistant team member to join the RtI team because she was a highly respected "veteran" teacher. The administrator was well aware this teacher had publicly stated opposition to the RtI process and on more than one occasion had said that she was near retirement and would be "long gone" before RtI was functional on the campus. The administrator thought that the staff development afforded to team members would change the teacher's attitude. What the administrator did not count on was that the teacher was not at all motivated to accept the change. Within the first six months of team development, the teacher became so disruptive to the process (by not collaboratively participating) that she was asked to leave the team. This caused problems with staff morale because the team was then perceived and promoted (by guess who) as an elitist group, which was not true. Typically, campus teachers will develop trust and respect for the team during the first year of RtI implementation, but because of the damage caused by this initial team selection, the RtI team on that campus needed two full years to gain acceptance and respect.

Organizing the Campus Team

When preparing to establish the campus RtI team, the campus principal must attend to details such as finding space for team meetings and file storage, purchasing supplies, and assigning a responsible person to help with duplication of forms. The principal should train all office staff on handling requests for campus RtI team assistance. The principal must also inventory resources available on the campus within classrooms (textbooks, technology, etc.), as well as school-wide resources, such as volunteers, peer tutoring, and availability of school psychologists, speech and language pathologists, social workers, physical therapists, and paraeducators. Additionally, any district-level supports that may be available, particularly with regard to staff development, should be evaluated. Finally, the principal must inventory resources available from the parents and within the community at large (such as after-school programs, support groups, community social programs, and tutoring). Parents are an important resource for schools because they know their children and their difficulties very well. Parents are vital in helping the team develop interventions.

paraeducators Support members of the learning and teaching team who ensure that students receive multiple levels of support in schools.

Once the team members have been selected and have received the initial RtI training, it is important for the principal to schedule weekly meeting times that are sacred (cannot be changed). The principal should publish these dates and distribute the schedule to staff and parents.

Now it is time to define the roles of the team members. The campus administrator is usually the chair of the team. Other roles can be standing for particular members, or they can be rotated per student case. Among the many ways to clarify specific roles, the following are the most common:

Chairperson: In most instances, the campus administrator chairs the team. The chairperson is primarily responsible for running the team's meetings and following a meeting agenda. The chair is responsible for the entire meeting process, including making sure that parents have been contacted and informed, but may choose to appoint a team member to be in charge of sending out notices and preparing the team for the meeting. During the meeting itself, the chairperson welcomes all in attendance, reviews the purpose of the meeting, and sets goals for the meeting. Next, the chair presents the concerns in terms of the data collected, guides the team in the problem-solving process, and supports the team in developing academic and behavioral strategies and the final intervention plan. Finally, the chairperson closes the meeting with a summary of the meeting discussion and agreed-upon plan and sets a time for the team to reconvene to discuss student progress. Outside of meetings, the chair responds to those who wish to refer a student and supplies them with preliminary information about the documentation the team will need. Additionally, the chairperson checks with the case manager on a regular basis to ensure that all processes are being followed with fidelity.

Timekeeper: The person in this position helps all members stay focused, by using timing techniques and bringing staff back to topic when discussions stray. The timekeeper holds the team to its schedule within meetings and gives updates on progress within the time limits as needed.

Case manager: This person is someone who can consult and collaborate with all staff to ensure fidelity of assessments and interventions. The case manager meets with the referring teacher to determine if resource allocation is sufficient, necessary materials are available, and support personnel for interventions are showing up at designated times. The case manager has a responsibility to the student, the parents, and the RtI team for ensuring that the process is going as planned, including helping the teacher of record and the designated interventionist make sure that all documentation forms are completed in a timely manner.

Document facilitator: This person is mainly responsible for documenting all aspects of the RtI team process, beginning at Tier 2. The document facilitator helps the referring teacher collate previous Tier 1 data and becomes primarily responsible for the processes of data collection and documentation that begin in Tier 2. This person might not be the one to carry out the assessments but is the one who ensures that they are documented correctly. This facilitator is also responsible for taking meeting minutes and notes, filling out required forms, and organizing all RtI team documents.

Critical to problem solving are the forms used to document the fidelity of the RtI process. The following is an example of the flow of data collection:

Universal screening results and documentation
- Classroom observations
- Review of records
- Documentation of level of curriculum taught and instructional intervention
- Parent notification of concerns

RtI referral
- Parent notification of RtI meeting
- Teacher/staff notification of RtI meeting
- Problem identification form
- Student information form
- Documentation of classroom observations
- Documentation of problem-solving meeting
- Intervention plan/fidelity documentation
- Progress monitoring/CBM results
- Progress reports

Documentation of progress monitoring/CBM results
- Description of interventions
- Student work samples
- Follow-up documentation of fidelity
- Data for formal request for multidisciplinary assessment: health history, progress reports, and campus RtI team reports (minutes and notes)

Remember that the campus team's chairperson is responsible for checking with team case managers to make sure all forms are completed at the specified time in the process.

RtI District Fidelity Checklist

District team task	No	1. Investigating	2. Developing	3. Implementing
District team analyzes and provides research-based core curriculum.				Analysis Complete Curriculum Ordered Training Set
District team analyzes and schedules staff on research-based instruction.		Challenge - -time constraints - some training Scheduled		
District team develops training on research-based instructional interventions.				August Trainings are on Staff development Calendar
District team develops RtI process guidelines.			District team is in process of finalizing guidelines	
District team analyzes and supports allocation of support and resources.		Currently analysis is ongoing on resource allocations.		
District team chooses assessment procedures and determines cutoff scores, learning-rate norms, etc.			September dates Scheduled - Will decide cutoff scores after Fall tests.	
District team analyzes campus needs regarding assessment and intervention materials.		Currently district is Surveying administrators on campus interventions.		

RtI Action Plan Readiness Survey

In order to evaluate the readiness of implementing RtI on your campus, it is important to measure essential components needed for successful implementation. This survey is offered to guide you through the critical thinking and resource identification phase of determining next steps for your campus.

Directions: Complete the items by circling the answer that best describes your campus. When finished, identify areas you need to focus on using the RtI Team Action Form.

0	1	2	3
No knowledge	Some knowledge	Developing knowledge	Comprehensive knowledge

STAFF UNDERSTANDING

1. Administration supports RtI model.	0	1	②	3
2. Staff have been trained on IDEA 2004 and understand RtI philosophy.	0	①	2	3
3. Staff are accepting of RtI philosophy and are receptive to change.	⓪	1	2	3
4. Staff have an awareness of current resources available aligning with tier interventions.	0	①	2	3

TEAM DEVELOPMENT

1. Principal has process for selecting team members.	0	1	②	3
2. Campus has staff development in place for new team members.	0	①	2	3
3. All staff support the team members selected (high degree of credibility according to campus needs).	0	①	2	3
4. Team structure (roles and responsibilities) is in place.	⓪	1	2	3
5. Guidelines are in place for referral, interventions, documentation.	⓪	1	2	3
6. Team uses a problem-solving approach during meetings.	⓪	1	2	3
7. School-wide resources are inventoried and available to team (academic and behavioral).	0	①	2	3
8. Documentation of interventions and follow-up are established.	⓪	1	2	3
9. Parents understand process and are regarded as active participants.	⓪	1	2	3

PROCEDURES DEVELOPED / INTERVENTIONS /ASSESSMENTS

1. Policies are developed and aligned with forms for documentation.	0	1	②	3
2. Procedures are developed for continuous staff development on research-based interventions (academic and behavior).	0	①	2	3
3. Staff are supported with resources.	0	1	②	3
4. Results of data collection are shared on a continuous basis with staff, parents, and administrators.	0	①	2	3
5. Staff are given continuous feedback on fidelity of assessments.	⓪	1	2	3
6. Staff are given continuous feedback on fidelity of interventions.	⓪	1	2	3

RtI Team Action Plan

Objectives	Proposed activities	Responsible person(s)	Timeline	Date completed
Staff understanding of model	Trainings needed: - IDEA 2004 - RtI Campus Survey of Resources	Campus LSSP/ Diagnostician District RtI Team Grade level teams	Aug. 15, 2008 Aug. 15, Oct 10, Dec. 8, 2008 Sept. 23, 2008	
Team development	Principal Selects Team New Team (campus) Training Develop team Structure (Roles) Parent training	Principal with Support of District RtI team District RtI Team Principal Campus RtI Team	July 25, 2008 Aug 14, continuos Aug. 14, 2008 Dec. 10, 2008	
Procedures developed	District Policies training Staff training	District RtI Team Principal	Aug. 1, 2008 Sept. 29, 2008	
Interventions trained and available	Identify Interventions Select Resource Staff Staff training	RtI District team Principal Principal	July 10, 2008 Aug. 15, 2008 Throughout year	
Assessment trained and implemented	Staff training Fidelity Checklist	Assessment Personnel Campus RtI Team	Aug 15, 2008 Ongoing	
Intervention and data collection monitored for fidelity	Staff Training Fidelity checklist	Trained Personnel Campus RtI Team	ongoing ongoing	

RtI Campus Fidelity Checklist

Campus team task	No	1. Investigating	2. Developing	3. Implementing
Administrator provides support to teachers for research-based core curriculum.				Curriculum ordered – Training has begun and is scheduled
Administrator surveys staff for professional development needs.			Staff surveys have been completed and are in the process of analysis.	
Administrator schedules staff development (RtI team process and staff understanding of RtI).		Principal is reviewing staff needs to determine "next steps" for staff development.		
Administrator provides staff with resources needed to ensure that RtI process is viable.		Principal is reviewing resources surveys, staff needs.		
Administrator conducts checks of fidelity of implementation.	Has not begun in a formal manner.			
Administrator is active participant on campus RtI team.			Principal has attended first 2 meetings and is supportive.	
Administrator communicates process to parents.			Principal discussed RtI at beg. of year PTO mtg. in August.	
Administrator monitors all data collection.			Campus is still developing assessment (CBM).	

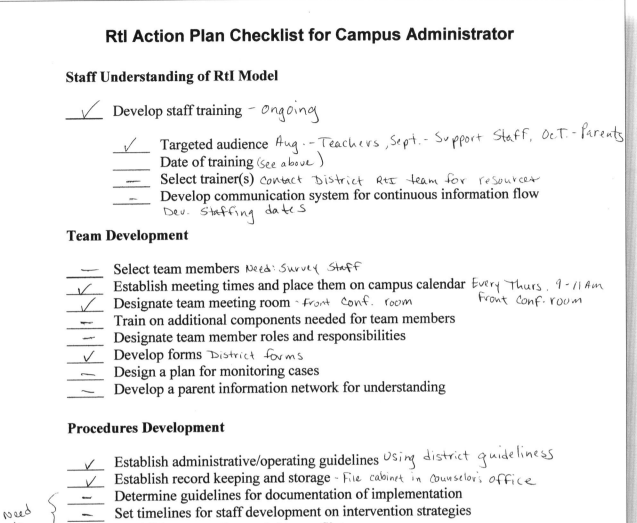

RtI Action Plan Checklist for Campus Administrator

Staff Understanding of RtI Model

✓ Develop staff training — *Ongoing*

   ✓ Targeted audience *Aug. — Teachers, Sept. — Support Staff, Oct. — Parents*
   ____ Date of training *(see above)*
   — Select trainer(s) *Contact District RtI team for resources*
   — Develop communication system for continuous information flow
        Dev. Staffing dates

Team Development

   — Select team members *Need: Survey Staff*
   ✓ Establish meeting times and place them on campus calendar *Every Thurs. 9-11 Am*
   ✓ Designate team meeting room — *Front Conf. room*   *Front Conf. room*
   — Train on additional components needed for team members
   — Designate team member roles and responsibilities
   ✓ Develop forms *District forms*
   — Design a plan for monitoring cases
   — Develop a parent information network for understanding

Procedures Development

   ✓ Establish administrative/operating guidelines *Using district guideliness*
   ✓ Establish record keeping and storage — *File cabinet in Counselor's office*
   — Determine guidelines for documentation of implementation   *Need to develop*
   — Set timelines for staff development on intervention strategies
   — Establish process for resolving conflicts

Other:

RtI Curriculum-Based Measurement Questions

1. What do you already know about progress monitoring and curriculum-based measurement (CBM)? What are you initial impressions?

   I have heard we will be using this assessment, but I have not used it. My initial impression is I am fearful it will take too much time to do, and I prefer to be teaching instead of testing. I am not sure how this assessment will help me teach struggling students.

2. Do you already use CBM strategies? Do you incorporate CBM strategies with other intervention methodologies?

   No

3. What would you like to learn about CBM and the Response to Intervention process?

   1. Why do we have to do it?
   2. What additional Information will it give me?
   3. How will it change the way we intervene with struggling learners?
   4. Do I have to do this?

RtI Implementation Guidelines for Problem Solving

1. **Gather information.**
    a. Appointed RtI team member meets with teacher and explains process.
    b. Teacher provides referral information supporting indicators (emotional and behavioral) of struggling learners, as well as academic data (benchmarks, student progress, Tier 1 interventions in place, and outcomes).

2. **Identify the problem.**
    a. Appointed team member establishes baseline data using CBM.
    b. Appropriate staff member (e.g., school psychologist, counselor, social worker) consults regarding emotional or behavioral issues.
    c. Focus on the problem, not the solution—describe problem(s) in objective, measurable terms.
    d. Rank-order concerns, and set measurable goals based on learning-rate norms.

3. **Brainstorm solutions.**
    a. Discuss district resources aligned with specific research-based strategies that could be used with identified problem(s).
    b. Encourage input from all team members, including parents.
    c. Generate as many solutions as possible.

4. **Evaluate interventions.**
    a. Identify strategies to be used (modify or combine brainstormed solutions).
    b. Check for referring teacher's agreement.
    c. Use collaborative feedback and shared decision-making.

5. **Choose intervention strategies.**
    a. Align strategies with appropriate tier (Tier 2 or 3).
    b. Review criteria for determining acceptable progress.

6. **Develop action plan.**
    a. Designate who is responsible of implementing and monitoring each strategy.
    b. Establish timelines, and set follow-up meeting time.
    c. Monitor intervention effectiveness using data from continuous progress monitoring (CBM and behavioral measures).
    d. Continue, modify, or add interventions based on student progress data.

RtI Decision-Making Guide

TIER 1
Universal screening: fall, spring, winter

1. Cut-off score = 25th percentile.
2. Principal chairs a meeting with RtI team. Data analysis to identify trends in students falling below cutoff score. Consultation with teachers occurs regarding curriculum and instructional practices.
3. Teachers implement core curriculum and strategies for 6–8 weeks. Review classroom data and analyze progress of struggling learners with CBMs or classroom-based assessments.

   * *Decision point:* Identify students who continue to fall below cutoff score and demonstrate a lack of progress, falling within the bottom 10 percent of students based on district norms. Schedule RtI meeting to discuss their move to Tier 2.

TIER 2
Strategic interventions: 9–12 weeks; repeat

1. Use researched fluency learning rates (Fuchs, Deno, Shapiro, AIMSweb, etc.).
   - Establish baseline scores and develop aimline (goal).
   - Determine number of weeks of intervention, a 30-minute session 2 or 3 days per week.
   - Problem-solve intervention (standard protocol).
   - Assign case manager, assessment support, and intervention support.
   - Begin intervention.
   - Progress monitoring 2 times per week.

     * *Decision point:* Weeks 4–6. Use a 3- or 4-data-point decision rule to monitor progress, and problem-solve if intervention needs to be altered.

   - Continue intervention.

     * *Decision point:* Weeks 9–12. Reconvene RtI team, and analyze data. If learning rate improves according to aimline, continue intervention. If not, change intervention and monitor for a repeat of weeks 9–12 ; *or* if learning rate continues to fall significantly below that of peers (10th percentile), refer student to Tier 3.

TIER 3
Intensive interventions

1. Increase intensity of intervention to two 30-minute sessions per day, 5 days a week, conducted by trained support personnel. RtI team may also add to standard protocol interventions.
2. Increase progress monitoring to 3 times per week.

   * *Decision point*: Weeks 9–12. If learning rate increases, continue intervention. If learning rate does not increase or if intensity of intervention is judged to be long-term based upon resources, refer student for a comprehensive evaluation.

   * *Decision point:* IEP (individualized education plan) team convenes to review comprehensive evaluation and determine special education eligibility. If student is deemed eligible, IEPs are developed based on all data. Progress monitoring continues. Student receives Tier 1 and Tier 3 interventions.

Chapter 3

Tier 1

Supporting All Students through Universal Screening and Interventions

Response to Intervention is designed to support struggling learners both academically and behaviorally. It is important for all staff to understand that this support is the responsibility of general education. Each of the three tiers in the RtI model represents particular methods of assessment as well as interventions that increase with the needs of struggling learners (see figures 1.1–1.3).

RtI development within the district occurs over time. To start building RtI at the campus level, focus initially on Tier 1 assessments and interventions.

Tier 1 is the foundation of the RtI process and involves the least intensive level of intervention. All students receive Tier 1 support. This tier is best described as implementing core curriculum and positive behavior strategies that effectively support about 80 percent of the students in the district. The interventions implemented at this stage are meant to be preventive and proactive (identify problems, intervene with sound curriculum and instruction, and use research-based strategies to promote learning). Therefore, instructional variables (such as delivery of instruction by using graphic organizers or computer-assisted instruction), curricular variables (such as entry point into the curriculum skill level or choice of a particular skill to work on), school organization (such as grouping teachers into teams according to grade level or content area), and structural variables (such as class schedules and space available for additional instruction and intervention) are examined and modified to increase the probability of success within the general education classroom.

The philosophy guiding Tier 1 is that student success within the general education environment can be ensured by providing proactive instruction (research-based), effective teaching strategies that focus on individual learning styles, and supports for positive behavior. Underlying the philosophy is the knowledge that

preventive Refers to action (such as early intervention) undertaken to avoid failure.

proactive Refers to action that anticipates future needs or problems, such as putting supports in place to increase the probability of successful learning outcomes and positive behaviors in the classroom.

instructional variable A quantifiable event or circumstance related to the action, practice, or profession of teaching.

curricular variable A quantifiable event or circumstance related to the instruction of students in the schools.

structural variables Quantifiable events or circumstances related to a school system's pattern of organization.

prevention and early intervention are more time- and cost-efficient and more likely to succeed than remediation strategies, which typically occur after a problem is already established and has been identified. The RtI philosophy encourages supplying parents and teachers with resources that would ultimately meet the needs of all students.

Universal Screening for Academic and Behavioral Skills

As in all RtI tiers, assessment guides decision making about interventions in Tier 1. Referred to as universal screening (or school-wide screening), Tier 1 assessment is designed to evaluate academic and behavioral skills and identify students whose performance is not consistent with that of their peers. The fundamental question at this stage of RtI is whether or not the student should be considered a struggling learner. The ultimate goal of universal screening is to develop research-based instructional practices that minimize failure and maximize success for all students.

Universal screening begins early in the school year (in the fall), is given to *all* students, and is administered two additional times during the year (winter and spring). A good screening process will quickly identify which students to target for intervention and whether there are specific gaps between student learning and core instruction expectations. The screening will also identify which groups of students on the campus or within the district show the most and least student progress. This in turn will lead to identifying support that may be necessary for some teachers and students.

Universal screening can be curriculum-based measurements (CBMs, discussed in Chapter 4), district benchmark assessments, state-mandated tests, and other types of assessment that the district has identified as useful. Typically the fall data are collected in September, the winter data in January, and the spring data in April. The district should establish guidelines for cutoff scores that will guide decision making for interventions. (Note: It is recommended that the cutoff scores be established by district-level curriculum coordinators/specialists to ensure consistency across the district when making decisions at Tier 1. See "Identifying Struggling Learners from the Data," below, for a discussion of cutoff scores.)

It is important that the district-level RtI team establish the dates for universal screening and place them on the testing calendar. In addition, campus administrators must convey to their staff the necessity of both completing the universal screening on all students and documenting the results within the time designated. In my experience, the fidelity of the administration and reporting of the universal screening has varied on many campuses that were implementing this form of assessment. Teachers must understand that Tier 1 decision making cannot begin unless the data are complete, so all teachers must submit their full results at the required time.

> **Lessons Learned:** Several district campus-based teams administered universal screening on the designated date. However, when campus RtI teams met on the designated date to review the data, it became apparent that many teachers either had not screened all their students (some did not screen their special education or ESL students) or had not reported all their results on time. Because the screening data were incomplete, they could not be analyzed, resulting in a delay before a number of the teams could begin teacher consultation and Tier 1 additional supports.

School districts are currently conducting universal screenings. But often they do not use the resulting data to analyze core curriculum or instructional needs for the classroom or individual students. To accomplish this level of data interpretation for RtI, teachers may need additional supports and resources, which will become apparent as a district begins to analyze RtI implementation issues. Thus, the guiding philosophy of interpretation and use of the data from universal screening changes in the context of the RtI process.

> **Lessons Learned:** In several school districts that have begun piloting a three-tier model, many teachers have not used test data to their advantage, because of time issues and the complex way in which data were presented. One campus administrator reported that when she visited with her teachers regarding a campus assessment that was being piloted, she found that the teachers had given the assessment and received the results. However, not one teacher on the campus opened the instructional manual on how to use the results to guide decisions. All of the manuals were sitting on a shelf, neatly wrapped in their original cellophane packets. When the administrator questioned the teachers, they responded that the testing itself was so time-consuming and cumbersome that they did not have time to review the manual to learn how the data could be linked to teaching practices. This is why it is extremely important to set up a universal screening system that uses current district assessments, plus any other needed tests, to provide the necessary information in a teacher- and student-friendly way. Teachers also need to be trained in how to align the results to intervention strategies. *Critical point:* Do not assume that all staff are comfortable with interpreting universal screening data and linking it to appropriate instructional and behavioral strategies.

align   To reorganize and modify components as needed so that they form a unified system.

The RtI campus team responsibility at Tier 1 is to help teachers use screening data to evaluate individuals and groups on specific academic and behavioral skills (reading, writing, math, attendance, cooperation, tardiness, truancy, suspensions, and so on). Although screening data may not be as robust for identifying individual student problems as more-intensive assessments are, they yield valuable information about core curricular and behavioral expectations within the school system. The information serves three purposes (Batsche et al. 2005):

- Provides information useful for evaluating class performance and identifying needed teacher supports
- Identifies students who need further evaluation and increased intensity of intervention (Tier 2)
- Identifies students who may slip through the cracks at one level of assessment but be caught by another

What should be measured at the universal screening level?

- Effectiveness of core curriculum
- Required developmental and prerequisite skills
- Student background information
- Skills that are the building blocks for acquiring higher-order skills

When deciding which core curriculum variables to include in the screening, it is important to enlist district specialists in reading, writing, and math. Besides helping identify the skills to be screened, these specialists can inform the district-level RtI committee on state mandates and recommendations regarding assessment and intervention and how they are currently being implemented in the district. For example, the National Reading Panel for the Elementary and Secondary Education Act has identified the essential components of reading instruction as phonemic awareness, phonics, vocabulary development, reading fluency, oral reading skills, and reading comprehension skills. The reading specialists can review the current district-wide assessments and recommend changes to ensure that they measure these components. Data collected should then be linked with instructional outcomes at each grade level, based on reading skill acquisition.

Once the district-level team has aligned the screening tools to the curriculum, it must create guidelines for using them. This will provide the framework for campus teams to analyze the screening data in a way that points out core curriculum and teaching needs. There also needs to be a frank discussion on whether the curriculum and teaching strategies used in the classroom are research-based *and* are being consistently implemented as they were intended to be (that is, with fidelity). Quite often campus staff will make statements such as "We are already

phonemic awareness Awareness of the sounds of language and how they make up words and sentences.

phonics An instructional design that involves teaching children to read by connecting sounds with letters or groups of letters.

doing that." However, in reality the strategies being used are frequently not delivered in the manner in which they were designed.

> **Lessons Learned:** A review of Tier 1 data at one elementary campus uncovered weaknesses in reading comprehension for one subset of children with high socioeconomic risk factors. When the RtI team investigated the instructional design with this in mind, it found that all second-grade teachers were using the Plato Learning lab as an instructional strategy for reading skills. Further investigation revealed that although their students participated in the Plato Learning lab, the teachers were not consistently using the Plato program as it was designed. Instead, they were picking and choosing when it came to using the program, depending on their preferences and the time they had allotted for this instructional strategy. The result was that the students who clearly needed this strategy were not receiving it consistently or in the way it was designed to be used. Therefore the campus could not determine if this was a strategy that promoted reading fluency and comprehension as it was designed to do.

Plato Learning lab
An intervention designed to increase learning and teaching effectiveness by addressing the entire spectrum of academic needs within a classroom.

Instruments for Assessing Academic Skills

The best place to begin when choosing the screening assessment is to analyze the district-wide assessments that are currently in place. Typically states have mandated or recommended assessments in the early elementary grades for reading, math, and writing. Analyze the data derived from those assessments, and then add or subtract assessments as your curriculum specialists recommend.

The most important aspect of this analysis is that the district adopts assessments for *all* students that are consistent across *all* grade levels. Some states focus intensive interventions and assessments in reading for kindergarten through third grade because of the Reading First initiative outlined in NCLB. These tools need to be analyzed to determine how they can be extended to the higher grades.

Reading First initiative
A process whereby states and districts receive support from the federal government for applying scientifically based research to ensure that all children learn to read well by the end of third grade.

> **Lessons Learned:** A district decided to pilot an RtI process up to the junior high level (grades 6–8). As the secondary curriculum specialists analyzed the proposed universal screening, they realized that many of their junior high teachers were not using developmental skill progression as an indicator for instructional design. For example, although most of the teachers covered literature content and grammar, they were not teaching the mechanics of reading. It was immediately clear that the junior high teachers needed to screen for those

developmental skill progression The process of acquiring the basic skills necessary for learning to occur.

skills and evaluate the data so that they could develop precise reading instruction for struggling readers.

Next, the campus principal problem-solved with the secondary coordinator of language arts and decided to provide opportunities for those teachers to participate in summer staff development classes that focused, not only on the developmental aspects of reading, but also on assessment of those skills and how to interpret the data to see what changes in instruction were needed. This became a crucial discussion because if assessments drive instructional practices, they must focus on these prerequisite skills—even at the junior high level.

Some of the secondary language arts teachers were less than enthusiastic about participating in this training. The most frequent reason given for the lack of enthusiasm was "It is not my job to teach reading. That should have been done in elementary school!" To address this barrier to a shift in philosophy, the campus principal designed and provided resources and training opportunities to the teachers before moving forward. Although they were not initially motivated, the staff participated in the training and many reported later that they were using the new strategies they learned.

When choosing universal screening instruments, it is important to following some simple guidelines:

validity The degree to which a test measures what it was designed to measure.

- The assessment instrument ensures the validity of the information collected. (That is, it screens for particular skills to identify students who may be in danger of failing the subject area.)
- The assessment is research-based, per NCLB standards.
- The assessment is easy to administer.
- Teachers know how to administer the assessment and interpret the data. (If not, develop training sessions for the teachers.)
- The data are presented in an easy-to-follow format for decision making.

Lessons Learned: As districts in the process of developing an RtI system have analyzed their current assessment practices for collecting benchmark data, they have added curriculum-based measurements and criterion- or norm-referenced tests to the universal screening lists. Instruments that have been analyzed and adopted across many districts nationwide include, but are not limited to, the following:

Curriculum-based measurements (reading, math, writing)

- AIMSweb
- CBM Warehouse (reading and math CBM probe development)
- DIBELS (Dynamic Indicators of Basic Early Literacy Skills)
- STEEP (System to Enhance Educational Performance)

Norm/criterion-referenced assessments (reading)

- Bader Reading and Language Inventory, 5th edition
- Brigance Diagnostic Comprehensive Inventory of Basic Skills—Revised (CIBS-R)
- Comprehensive Test of Phonological Processing
- Developmental Reading Assessment, 2nd edition (DRA2) (Pearson Learning Group)
- Early Reading Diagnostic Assessment, 2nd edition (ERDA-2)
- Fox in a Box
- Gray Oral Reading Test, 4th edition (GORT-4)
- Iowa Test of Basic Skills (ITBS)
- An Observation Survey of Early Literacy Achievement, 2nd edition
- Phonological Awareness Literacy Screening (PALS 1–3)
- Pre-Reading Inventory of Phonological Awareness (PIPA)
- Rigby PM Ultra Benchmark Kit System (Harcourt Achieve)
- Rigby READS (Reading Evaluation and Diagnostic System; Harcourt Achieve)
- Stanford Achievement Test (SAT), 10th edition
- Stanford Diagnostic Reading Test (SDRT), 4th edition
- STAR Early Literacy Computer-Adaptive Diagnostic Assessment
- Texas Primary Reading Inventory (TPRI)
- Yopp-Singer Test of Phoneme Segmentation

norm-referenced assessment A measure of performance in terms of an individual's standing in some known group, such as all of a district's students at a particular grade level.

criterion-referenced assessment A measure of performance in terms of a clearly defined learning task.

Norm/criterion-referenced assessments (math)

These assessments focus on essential skills of mathematics education: numeracy, basic skills (knowledge and application), and problem solving (understanding and application)

- Everyday Mathematics Teacher's Assessment Assistant (Ventura Educational Systems)
- Group Mathematics Assessment and Diagnostic Evaluation (G-MADE)

Norm/criterion-referenced assessments (writing)

- Process Assessment of the Learner (PAL)
- Wechsler Individual Achievement Test, 2nd edition (WIAT-II) (Spelling, Written Expression)

Identifying Struggling Learners from the Data

A district's universal screening plan can be developed to compare students' performance with local norms or national norms, based on age or grade. If the district would like to use local norms, its screening system will need to gather all student scores, based on age or grade, and then arrange the data by percentile ranks. District specialists within each curricular area help identify which scores fall within the percentile that indicates struggling learners. This percentile then becomes the cutoff score used to identify struggling learners. If the district prefers, it can choose to use national scores that are criterion-referenced and often are reported as percentile or quartile scores. These scores represent a national sample of student performance that can be compared with district screening data to determine the cutoff score.

cutoff score Within RtI, a preset score set to help identify struggling learners during universal screening at Tier 1.

There is no universally accepted cutoff score. Rather, a cutoff score is usually designed to identify the bottom 15 to 20 percent of students at grade level, or if a state-mandated or recommended test or a nationally normed test is used, the cutoff is often defined as the 10th percentile score.

When analyzing universal screening data, administrators and the RtI team typically begin by looking for patterns within the classroom, campus, or district, where data suggest that more than 20 percent of the student population is falling below the cutoff score. The presiding philosophy at this stage is that if more than 20 percent of the students in the universal screening fall below the cutoff score, the reason is not a within-student issue. Instead, it may indicate that Tier 1 foundations of core curriculum and instruction need to be altered to meet the needs of the students. The data should be analyzed to determine whether the concerns are district-wide, school-wide, or classroom-based. *Be careful here.* This step is extremely important. All students should be judged against the same cutoff scores. Certain student populations—such as those with English as a second language (ESL), low-income students, and so on—should not be assigned a higher percentage rate of failure to meet cutoff standards. If the data show such a pattern, then the emphasis of RtI should be on redesigning the curriculum and instruction to meet the needs of the population.

within-student issue An issue that is due to a student's learning abilities.

Lessons Learned: One campus RtI team found that 35 percent of its ESL students performed below the identified cutoff score for first-grade expectations in reading. The data also revealed that the students were primarily showing deficits in the areas of phoneme segmentation, sound blending, and fluency. The RtI team then invited district- and campus-level reading specialists and a bilingual specialist to a meeting to evaluate the curriculum. The team examined instructional strands on the identified areas with respect to expected language learning rates, skill introduction, repeated drills, and supplemental teaching strategies and was able to pinpoint weaknesses in the instructional design. This resulted in designing staff training for understanding language as it relates to the development of reading skills, and adding research-based curriculum materials and bilingual teaching strategies for the general education teachers to use as Tier 1 supports for students. Upon the next review of universal screening data, the RtI team noted an upward trend in learning rates for the identified students, indicating that the added support in Tier 1 was having a positive effect.

Another example of using universal screening data to enhance Tier 1 supports happened at a campus where the demographics of the student population included low socioeconomic variables (poverty). The initial universal screening showed a large portion of the kindergarten and first-grade students falling below the designated cutoff scores in reading (approximately 38 percent). The RtI team analyzed the data and determined that many of the students might not have had a strong language experience to draw upon for language and reading development. The campus principal asked for support from the district speech pathologist, who immediately consulted with the kindergarten and first-grade teams. Together they developed lesson plans with increased language enrichment activities. The speech pathologist also went into the classrooms and modeled whole-class instructional strategies for the teachers to use to increase the language experience of the students. The RtI team noticed a significant increase in reading skills for the kindergarten and first-grade students upon reviewing the next set of universal screening data.

phoneme segmentation The ability to break up and identify the sounds within words.

sound blending The blending of sounds together to form words.

fluency An acceptable level of mastery of a skill.

After analyzing the data, the RtI team either rules out curriculum and teaching practices as causes of concern or else takes action to improve them where needed. Once that has been done, the RtI team can focus on the 15 to 20 percent of students who remain below the cutoff score. These students are then designated as struggling learners, and the classroom teacher will be given training and support to boost their learning.

Meanwhile, student progress should be monitored to determine if a higher level of intervention is needed (Tier 2). Once a child is identified as a struggling learner at Tier 1, monitoring should include consistency in the delivery of instruction, documentation of interventions, and rates of learning for 6 to 8 weeks. "Fidelity of instruction" simply means that the teachers are consistently carrying out the core curriculum and instructional strategies as they were designed. The RtI team should monitor both teacher support and student progress once a week to see whether the student makes progress as the teacher implements newly acquired skills in curriculum and instruction. If the student does not show academic gains within the designated time determined by the district guidelines (usually 6 to 8 weeks), then the RtI committee should talk with the teacher, review all documentation of interventions, and recommend either giving additional support to the teacher or moving the student to the Tier 2 level of assessment and interventions.

documentation Any material (such as student products, tests, written reports) containing data gathered during the RtI process.

Evaluating Behavioral Skills and Supports

In addition to academic skills, Tier 1 assessment also focuses on behavior. The initial district-level RtI team must determine which aspects of behavior will be assessed in Tier 1. Suggested screening measures include reviewing the following school records:

- Attendance
- Tardies
- Office referrals (note time of day, referring teacher, and setting where the behavior occurred)
- Disciplinary actions taken (parent call, detention, suspension)

Tier 1 data must include classroom/environment observations that note whether positive behavioral supports are in place, such as the following examples:

- Class rules are posted and visible.
- Positive and negative consequences are clear, immediately given, linked to behaviors, and consistently implemented.
- Social skills and character programs are introduced, modeled, and reinforced.
- Organization of learning areas (physical space designated for learning) is evident.
- Routines and schedules are clear.
- Study/learning strategies and teacher's expectations of students are taught.
- Active supervision and monitoring of students are evident.
- Discipline is enforced in a firm and fair manner.

Along with such observations, the district may also choose to purchase a student risk screening instrument that would be used with *all* students, such as one of these:

- California School Climate and Safety Survey
- Drummond's Student Risk Screening Scales (SRSS)
- School Motivation and Learning Strategies Inventory (SMALSI)
- Student Interaction in Specific Settings (SISS)

The assessment of behavior at Tier 1 is designed to focus on prevention and early intervention, using classroom and school-wide supports. It is much easier to support changes in behavior at this level. Behavioral interventions have a much higher rate of success when they are addressed early, at Tier 1.

Universal Academic Interventions

The RtI approach requires that the design of the Tier 1 interventions focus on how student learning is affected by a variety of instructional variables:

- The nature of the instruction (resources, materials, curriculum, and programs)
- The time allocated to the delivery of instruction (including guided practice of introduced skills)
- Prerequisite skills students have mastered prior to delivery of instruction
- The validity of the instructional practices
- The fidelity of the implementation of instructional strategies or programs

It is paramount that staff understand that the purpose of this approach is not to determine student eligibility for special programs or services. Rather, the focus is on designing and implementing effective instructional practices. As mentioned earlier, the goal of universal screening is to develop research-based instructional practices that minimize failure and maximize success for all students. The greater the needs of the learner, the greater the demand on instructional design and implementation. The core academic program needs to be evaluated to determine whether the instruction provided on the essential elements is designed to meet the needs of most of the students. Once the academic program has been shown to be meeting those needs, additional instructional strategies will focus on the particular needs of some of the students. (Remember, one size does not fit all.) At this level of intervention, the

differentiated instruction An approach to teaching and learning in which students have multiple options for taking in information and making sense of ideas; requires teachers to be flexible in adjusting their methods and the curriculum to suit students, rather than expecting students to modify themselves for the curriculum.

focus is on targeting essential skills, supporting differentiated instructional practices, monitoring student responses, and training teachers in critical skills.

Universal instruction focuses on *all* learners by using interventions that focus on assessment, research-based strategies, and skills development of both students and teachers. By receiving training, teachers and staff become skilled in planning and implementing research-based instructional practices that include curriculum, delivery of instruction, and positive behavior support systems. The NCLB Act defines "scientifically based research" for the education community:

The term "scientifically based research"—

(A) means research that involves the application of rigorous, systematic, and objective procedures to obtain reliable and valid knowledge relevant to education activities and programs; and

(B) includes research that—

(i) employs systematic, empirical methods that draw on observation or experiment;

(ii) involves rigorous data analyses that are adequate to test the stated hypotheses and justify the general conclusions drawn;

(iii) relies on measurements or observational methods that provide reliable and valid data across evaluators and observers, across multiple measurements and observations, and across studies by the same or different investigators;

(iv) is evaluated using experimental or quasi-experimental designs in which individuals, entities, programs, or activities are assigned to different conditions and with appropriate controls to evaluate the effects of the condition of interest, with a preference for random-assignment experiments, or other designs to the extent that those designs contain within-condition or across-condition controls;

(v) ensures that experimental studies are presented in sufficient detail and clarity to allow for replication or, at a minimum, offer the opportunity to build systematically on their findings; and

(vi) has been accepted by a peer-reviewed journal or approved by a panel of independent experts through a comparably rigorous, objective, and scientific review.

random-assignment experimental design An experimental technique in which subjects randomly receive different treatments (or no treatment).

within-condition experimental design An experimental technique in which the same subjects are tested on a single condition.

across-condition control design An experimental technique in which different conditions are measured using the same subjects.

The district-level RtI team will usually devote many discussions to this topic initially. It is crucial that the team embrace these criteria for research-based instructional practices, because they will become the foundation for accurate assessment of Tier 1 education by campus personnel. Several publications and supports related to research-based curriculum, strategies, and training are available at these websites: the U.S. Department of Education (www.ed.gov), the What Works Clearinghouse (ies.ed.gov/ncee/wwc/), Intervention Central (www.interventioncentral.org), and the Florida Center for Reading Research (www.fcrr.org).

There has been much confusion and anxiety regarding where to find good research-based strategies for Tier 1 supports. The district-level RtI team is responsible for preparing guidelines that campus teams can follow when selecting Tier 1 supports that meet the NCLB research-based standards. The best way to accomplish this is for the curriculum specialists on the district team to inventory past staff development in the district, as well as the strategies that have been stressed within the instructional design of general education (such as training on differentiated instruction, multiple intelligences, and so on). Once the curriculum specialists identify these strategies, the district team can design a Tier 1 reference guide for staff development that will lead the campus teams to research-based strategies and supports. Often teachers want a "checklist" of strategies or a binder of programs to guide them through Tier 1, but it is critical that all staff and parents understand that Tier 1 supports are focused on good instructional design and delivery and not on a particular program. Therefore I do not recommend that teachers be given a "checklist" or binder of particular programs; instead, the campus team should guide teachers to the research-based practices through effective consultation and staff development, as identified by the district-level team.

An important aspect of instruction is the delivery skills necessary for improving the achievement levels of all learners. It is no mystery that maximizing instructional time highly correlates with increased learning. When implementing Tier 1, make sure that teachers get the support they need for optimizing their time in the classroom so that they can accomplish the following:

- Increase opportunities to respond within the context of the lesson.
- Increase opportunities to build on prior knowledge and enhance success within the content being discussed.
- Alter the instruction delivery so that the pace is appropriate.
- Differentiate the instruction to increase the opportunity for all learners to understand.

Therefore, scheduling of instruction, student grouping (cooperative learning opportunities), and delivery of instruction are the focuses of Tier 1 intervention, along with analysis of the core curriculum.

Teachers will need a variety of supports for implementing Tier 1 in their classrooms. Essential to increasing student achievement is the notion that the core curriculum is research-based *and* delivered consistently on a daily basis. In addition to receiving training, teachers must be given the time to deliver the needed instruction to their students. To achieve this, the administration staff, teaching staff, and consulting specialists must coordinate their efforts. Along with the core curriculum, teachers will be presenting optimal opportunities to students with a variety of needs in Tier 1. To gain the knowledge and resources for doing this, teachers must have access to consultants in relevant areas of specialization (for example, dyslexia, bilingual, behavior, and so on).

When supporting struggling learners in Tier 1, teachers will need information about the skills students need for progressing in the curriculum, particularly in reading and math. Reading is easier to address because the NCLB Reading First initiative provides guidelines and expectations for increasing student reading proficiencies in five areas: phonemic awareness, phonics, vocabulary, fluency, and comprehension. Addressing mathematics is more complicated because there has not been an extensive, coordinated research effort in this content area. Rather, the research has been isolated for certain skills. The good news is that all states provide academic standards for development of math skills. According to the National Council of Teachers of Mathematics, which is often used as a resource for effective mathematics instruction, basic skills should be in conjunction with reasoning, problem solving, technology, and cross-disciplinary alignment. A valuable resource for examining essential mathematical skills is *Adding It Up: Helping Children Learn Mathematics,* which was published by the Mathematics Learning Study Committee of the National Research Council (Kilpatrick, Swafford, and Findell 2001).

To ensure high-quality instruction, staff development should focus on specific skill strategies in the content areas as well as on the art of differentiating instruction. Teachers may need instruction, modeling, and feedback on how to increase academic instruction through flexible grouping, scheduling, and accommodation of different student learning styles. Since differentiated instruction strategies also rely on self-motivation, teacher training must include techniques for helping students develop intrinsic motivation.

Resources that may help teachers become proficient in selecting research-based instruction and strategies include, but are not limited to, the following:

learning style The method of learning, individualized to a student, that allows the student to learn most easily and effectively.

intrinsic motivation Motivation that is governed by an individual's internal drives.

Reading

- Corrective Reading (McGraw-Hill)
- Guided Reading (Heinemann Press)
- Harcourt Reading/Language Arts Program
- Literacy Place (Scholastic)
- Open Court (SRA/McGraw-Hill)
- Peer-Assisted Learning Strategies (PALS; Vanderbilt Kennedy Center for Research on Human Development)
- Reading Rockets

- Rigby Literacy (Harcourt Rigby Education)
- Success for All
- Trophies (Harcourt School Publishers)

Math

- Accelerated Math (Renaissance Learning)
- Connected Mathematics (Prentice Hall)
- Every Day Counts: Calendar Math (Great Source/Houghton Mifflin)
- Everyday Mathematics (SRA/McGraw-Hill)
- Peer-Assisted Learning Strategies (PALS; Vanderbilt Kennedy Center for Research on Human Development)

Strategies

- Concept Mapping
- "Curriculum and Instruction for All Abilities and Intelligences" (Fisher 2000)
- "Differentiating Cooperative Learning" (Schniedewind and Davidson 2000)
- "Differentiating Instruction for Advanced Learners in the Mixed-Ability Middle School Classroom" (Tomlinson 1995)
- EduScapes (www.eduscapes.com)
- "Inspired Investigations" (McKenzie 2003)
- "Intrinsic Motivation" (Theroux; members.shaw.ca/priscillatheroux/motivation.html)
- Learning Styles
- "Mixed Ability Teaching: Problems and Possibilities" (Reid et al. 1981)

Universal Behavioral Interventions

Universal behavioral interventions are meant to be delivered campus-wide. The interventions center on classroom and building supports that help students respond positively to their environment. These supports include developing consistent classroom and school-wide rules and routines, teaching and modeling behavioral expectations, administering consequences fairly and consistently (both positive and negative), and ensuring that teachers are delivering effective instruction in their classrooms.

Positive behavioral supports are not a new concept. Many states require them as a part of the campus plan. Administrators and teachers must understand that positive behavioral supports are not a specific curriculum (although some excellent curricula support the system) and are not limited to a particular group of students. Effective behavioral supports in the school setting are foundational—they focus on the classroom and other specific settings (such as buildings, playgrounds, and buses) and on individual student needs. The campus administrator must analyze the universal screening data to ensure that the foundational pieces of behavioral supports are in place. If the data indicate gaps, they are then addressed through staff development.

prosocial behaviors
Actions that are intended to benefit others in social situations.

Lessons Learned: When a campus principal reviewed screening data at her elementary school, she found that four teachers generated 80 percent of the discipline referrals sent to her office. The principal and the RtI team conducted classroom observations and noted that classroom rules were not posted or reinforced, schedules and routines varied in the classrooms, positive incentives were not consistently given, negative consequences far outnumbered the positives, and students did not receive instructions or modeling of appropriate prosocial behaviors. The principal scheduled brief trainings on behavioral foundations for the teachers (three 45-minute trainings) led by the district's school psychologist. Training included developing classroom rules, using precision commands, and creating positive reinforcement systems in the classroom. Subsequent data collection showed a decrease in office referrals in all four classrooms.

Interventions that are proactive for behavior support include these:

Rules

- Predetermined, written, and posted
- Taught for at least the first 5 weeks of school
- Consistently monitored, with feedback for teachers
- Consistently enforced

Routines and daily schedules

- Posted
- Consistently followed
- Consistently taught

Consequences

- Predetermined
- Taught and arranged for more chances of receiving a positive support (*Rule of thumb:* Students should receive 5 positive consequences for every negative consequence delivered.)
- Meaningful to the students (age appropriate)
- Given consistently and privately

Environment

- Organized
- Efficient
- Designed for maximum focus of attention
- Designed to increase student-teacher interactions

The most important aspect of universal behavioral interventions is related to teacher skills in the areas of designing organized classrooms (seating), setting schedules that are conducive to learning and behaviors (such as timing of instruction, seating, built-in breaks), managing the instruction by using groups and the environment, providing direct instructions regarding behavioral expectations that are tied to rules and social skills/character development, and implementing a good system of positive and negative consequences. A number of positive behavioral support systems offer direction for developing excellent school-wide structures, including, but not limited to, these two:

- CHAMPs (Sprick 1998)
- Project Achieve

These additional resources related to universal behavioral supports are also recommended:

- National Association of School Psychologists (NASP) (www.nasponline .org)
- National Technical Assistance Center on Positive Behavioral Supports (www.pbis.org)
- Office of Special Education and Rehabilitative Services (OSERS) (www.ed.gov/about/offices/list/osers)
- Safe and Civil Schools (www.safeandcivilschools.com)

Fidelity of Implementation

A district can go through the Tier 1 process of evaluating research-based instruction and design as put forth by the No Child Left Behind Act, but without fidelity of implementation (consistency of instruction and interventions) there will not be improved results for struggling learners. "Fidelity of implementation" simply means carrying out an instructional program in the manner in which it was designed. The RtI campus team will not be able to analyze data and provide supports if it cannot determine the appropriateness of the instruction within the classroom. Therefore it is crucial that the district provide staff development in the areas of assessment, instruction, and intervention to ensure fidelity.

Suggested practices to develop fidelity can be found at the National Research Center for Learning Disabilities (NRCLD) website (www.nrcld.org). Basically the district-level team must clearly outline the assessments to be used in the RtI process; devise a user-friendly format for presenting the data; articulate the interventions endorsed by the district; create a system for analyzing the data; and outline methods for accountability (particularly when intervention noncompliance occurs). According to the National Joint Committee on Learning Disabilities (2005), a three-dimensional model for fidelity of implementation includes providing a variety of tools for delivering information to staff; frequently checking to ensure fidelity; and using feedback and staff development to provide staff with the support they need to be successful.

The district-level RtI teams must develop fidelity checklists or action plans as guidelines for campus staff. Many good checklists are available that the district-level team can review for incorporation into its policies. One recommended website to consult is www.interventioncentral.org. Its *RTI_WIRE* section contains forms created by the School-Based Intervention Team (SBIT) Project, in addition to providing links to models developed by an assortment of states and local school districts. Also see the fidelity checklist forms for both district and campus provided here on pages 25 and 28, as well as the RtI Classroom Fidelity Checklist on page 52.

To ensure monitoring effectiveness, it is very important to track consistency of implementation and staff behaviors as they relate to the design of the intervention and data collection. After the district-level team designs the fidelity checklists, campus administrators will use them to guide the campus RtI team in deciding who will monitor the instruction and interventions and in developing appropriate forms for monitoring. See, for example, the RtI Team Documentation of Instruction and Interventions forms for reading, math, and behavior and the RtI Classroom Observation Form on pages 53–56.

Generally speaking, when choosing the monitoring person, the team needs to evaluate who is trained in the specific area of instruction (reading, math, behavior), instructional strategy used, or intervention that is being observed. To ensure the validity of the observational data, the team must select a person who has been trained in structured observation techniques. The monitor must also possess effective consultation skills for providing positive corrective feedback to staff. And finally, the monitor must be someone the staff views with mutual respect.

It is crucial that staff be aware that this type of monitoring will occur as part of the RtI process and that it will be consistently implemented across all grades and teachers. When discussing the issue of monitoring for fidelity, the campus administrator needs to reassure the staff that this technique is part of designing high-quality supports and services and is *not* a punitive process. The staff need to be assured that the feedback is always given to the teacher in a collaborative manner after an observation and that it will be shared with the RtI team during its next regularly scheduled meeting.

structured observation technique A formal method of observing students and the environment.

RtI Classroom Fidelity Checklist

Classroom task	No	1. Investigating	2. Developing	3. Implementing
Teacher uses research-based core curriculum.				
Teacher implements research-based instructional strategies.				
Teacher uses data to ensure instructional matching.				
Teacher implements standard protocol interventions as designed.				
Teacher implements and interprets universal screening data.				
Teacher understands and uses CBM data to drive problem solving.				
Teacher participates in RtI process as guidelines suggest.				
Teacher seeks out professional development as needed.				

RtI Team Documentation of Instruction and Interventions: Reading

Student Name __George M.__   Teachers __Smith, Lawrence, Jones__

Date of Birth __9/11/99__   Grade __3__

Targeted Area of Intervention	Interventions	Consistency of Implementation (Lesson plans, observations, and attendance)	Fidelity Check (Adherence to program design)
Phonemic Awareness	Not Targeted as intervention. George demonstrates adequate progress using district reading curriculum.	Lesson Plans incorporating district curriculum (Houghton-Mifflin) (used daily)	Lesson Plans documented. Fidelity of district curriculum instruction.
Phonics	Not Targeted as intervention. George demonstrates adequate progress.	Lesson Plans incorporating district curriculum (Houghton-mifflin) (used daily)	See Above
Fluency	Provide George books on independent reading level (2.0). Use word cards (blends, rimes). Provide Peer Partner to model and practice reading.	Lesson Plans incorporating 15 min. daily independent reading. Word cards provided daily with 90% accuracy. Peer reading dyad 15 min. daily.	Observations and teacher interviews do not support consistent daily implementation. (scheduling conflicts) ✗
Vocabulary	Not Targeted - vocabulary is not impacted by fluency deficiencies.	Lesson Plans building grade-level vocabulary skills. (used daily).	Lesson Plans documented Fidelity of district curriculum instruction.
Comprehension	Provide George with books on independent level. Discuss characters in story - Ask who, what, why questions. Have George to discuss supporting details	Reading specialist will incorporate comprehension strategies 3 times per week during small group instruction (30 minutes per session).	Observations and reading Specialist document fidelity of intervention.
Writing	Not Targeted.	Lesson Plans document writing activities as part of ECA instruction.	Observations and lesson plans document fidelity of instruction.

We assure that the above noted intervention(s) were conducted as disclosed.

_____   _____   _____
Principal   Teacher Service Provider   RTI Team Member

RtI Team Documentation of Instruction and Interventions: Math

Student Name ___Sarah S.___ Teachers ___Dolly Abrams (math)___

Date of Birth ___11 / 2 / 2007___ Grade ___2___

Targeted Area of Intervention	Interventions	Consistency of Implementation (Lesson plans, observations, and attendance)	Fidelity Check (Adherence to program design)
Math Concepts	Sarah demonstrates difficulty with base ten concepts, particularly using place value. She will be grouped homogeneously with 2 peers for 3 sessions per week on small group instruction (20 min. per session).	Lesson plans incorporate scaffolding, "think aloud," and errorless learning during differentiated instruction. Math Specialist documentation of small group instruction 3 times per week (20 minutes).	Lesson plans document daily activities; however teacher was absent 5 days and substitute did not consistently implement. * math specialist documentation indicates consistent implementation for all sessions.
Math Computation	Procedural difficulties in strategy use and execution will be addressed in small group instruction with 2 peers for 3 sessions per week (15 minutes). Sarah will also be assigned a daily peer buddy for independent practice (15 minutes per day).	Lesson plans document differentiated instruction and use of cooperative grouping strategies. Peer buddy assigned was present for all opportunities daily. (Attendance = 100%).	See above. Peer buddy is consistent (observations). Math specialist missed 3 sessions due to scheduling conflicts. *

We assure that the above noted intervention(s) were conducted as disclosed.

_____ _____ _____
Principal Teacher Service Provider RTI Team Member

RtI Team Documentation of Instruction and Interventions: Behavior

Student Name _Harry H._

Date of Birth _4/10/97_

Teachers _S. Reaves, P. Smith_

Grade _4_

Targeted Area of Intervention	Interventions	Consistency of Implementation (Lesson plans, observations, and attendance)	Fidelity Check (Adherence to program design)
Behavior / Classroom Management	Preferential seating to allow for proximity control. Classroom is highly organized. Use of graphic organizers paired with frequent feedback.	Harry has been in attendance 98% of the time. Teacher documentation of assigned seating along with scheduled lessons indicates the use of graphic organizers and preferential seating.	Classroom observations and structured feed-back indicate consistent implementation.
Behavior Action Plan / Positive Behavior Supports	Positive Behavior Supports: 1. lottery ticket system tied to on-task behaviors 2. positive verbal praise for task engagement and completion.	- Good attendance (see above) - Behavior chart tied to lottery system is used for documentation	Documentation on behavior charts and observations indicate fidelity.
Social Skills, Resiliency Training, Character Education	Small group social skills training in a "Lunch Bunch" group with counselor.	Lesson plans have been developed using the "Tough Kids" Social Skills curriculum.	Observations indicate the instruction has been implemented as scheduled. Harry also participated in structured role play.

We assure that the above noted intervention(s) were conducted as disclosed.

_____   _____   _____
Principal   Teacher Service Provider   RTI Team Member

RtI Classroom Observation Form

Student Name _Sarah Smith_ Observer Name _Kendall Jones_

Teacher/Subject _Dolly Abrams_ Class Size _23_ Date _12/7/07_

Time In _8:45 Am_ Time Out _9:05_ Task/Activity _Direct Instruction (Math Concepts)_

Time on Task Sample (Using 30-second timed intervals, circle + if student is engaged with task at time of observation, and circle – if not engaged.

1	2	3	4	5	6	7	8	9	10	11	12	13	14	15	16	17	18	19	20
⊕	⊕	⊕	⊕	⊕	+	+	+	+	⊕	⊕	⊕	⊕	⊕	⊕	⊕	⊕	⊕	⊕	⊕
–	–	–	–	–	⊖	⊖	⊖	⊖	–	–	–	–	–	–	–	–	–	–	–

Looking out window

↳ T. redirect

Delivery of Instruction _Ms. Abrams used graphic organizers on board; overhead projector; Introduced concepts using concept maps with verbal directives._

Use of Accommodations _Sarah was seated in first seat, middle row, next to projector. Sarah was also assigned a peer tutor._

Teacher Feedback _None observed (directed to Sarah)_

Peer Behaviors _Peer attention was commensurate with Sarah. Peers quiet and on-task_

Other _N/A_

Student Behaviors (N = not observed, S = sometimes, O = often)

Helped by Peer →

Eyes oriented to task	O	Fidgeting in seat	S
Listens to directions	O	Looking around room	S
Interacts with teacher	N	Careless /quick response	N
Working 1/1 with teacher	N	Plays with materials	N
Engaged in independent task	S	Stares blankly	N
Small group	N	Doodles	N
Area organized	O	Makes noises	N
Volunteers answer	N	Talks out of turn	N
Follows 1-step directions	O	Disorganized materials	N
Follows 2-step directions	O	Slow to respond	S
Follows _3_-step directions	S	Noncompliant	N
Responds to positive praise	N	Out of seat	N
Copies from OH/board	O	Argues with peers	N
Other_____		Other_____	

When called upon, gives correct answer Y (N)

Attends to other students when they give answers (Y) N

Knows appropriate place in text (Y) N

Facilitates others in group/class Y (N)

Completes assignment within required time (Y) N

Work is accurate (Y) N

Observed introduced curriculum level _3.4_ (on-level)

Chapter 4

Tier 2
Matching Student Needs with Effective Intervention Strategies

In Tier 1 of RtI, intervention is based on universal screening and is provided through whole-class instruction and support. This level of intervention is applied to all students and is considered the least intensive for individual support. Tier 1 focuses on the curriculum, instruction, and environment within the general education classroom.

During Tier 1 interventions, the learning rate of students is monitored by universal screening, student products, and classroom observation. Students are identified as struggling learners based on these data and on documentation of the fidelity of research-based instruction, design, and strategies. The campus RtI team supports teacher efforts through feedback, training, and other resources.

After receiving Tier 1 interventions, some students typically continue to struggle academically and/or behaviorally. Their learning rate falls below the preset cutoff score on universal benchmark data and data generated by the teacher (student products such as completed worksheets, homework, and projects; classroom observations; and teacher-made tests). For these students, the next step is to refer them for Tier 2 support.

In Tier 2 the interventions become student-centered and are individually tailored to meet the struggling student's needs. The Tier 2 process relies on problem solving by the campus RtI team, which bases its decisions on assessments of student progress.

The Problem-Solving Process

The problem-solving process for intensifying student-based interventions begins at Tier 2. A good way to think of this phase is in terms of the student support teams of the past that addressed referrals for struggling learners. The main differ-

student-based interventions
Interventions specifically designed for individual students.

ence in the RtI process is that this stage is *not* considered a step toward special education eligibility. Instead, Tier 2 focuses on intervening early, before a problem becomes substantial.

It is important for parents and staff to understand that RtI is a general-education process and is not designed to categorize children into programs or to assign labels that define the problems or interventions. Rather, the Tier 2 process defines the problem objectively (as specific skill deficits in academics and/or behavior), uses the problem-solving method to create a plan of research-based interventions, collects data systematically, and evaluates the effectiveness of the plan.

The campus RtI team becomes actively involved in the problem-solving process as soon as a student is referred for Tier 2 intervention. Parents, staff, an administrator, or the campus RtI team may refer a student to this next stage of intervention. A referral to Tier 2 should be based on data collected in Tier 1. These data must demonstrate that the student has already received an appropriate research-based curriculum and supports.

It is critical that decisions for moving students between Tier 1 and Tier 2 be consistently applied. It is very easy to base decisions on emotions rather than data. Campus RtI teams work for the best interest of the child, and it is only human that emotions affect decision making. Thus it is essential that the campus team be highly trained in the problem-solving process and adhere to the guidelines established by district RtI team. (See Chapter 2 for details of establishing and training campus teams and developing guidelines for them.)

Lessons Learned: In the past, student support teams may have based their decisions on emotions (teacher frustration, parent concerns, student struggles), particularly when teachers believed they had tried everything they knew and nothing worked. To determine whether a past decision was based on emotions or data, a team can look over the documentation to see whether it recorded opinions or data. Basing decisions on emotions can be detrimental because the supports chosen for a student may be misguided, causing important interventions to be delayed.

An example of this occurred when one campus used a pre-referral student support team model for a particular student. The team referred the student to a psychologist for testing to determine whether the student was eligible for special education. The team documented its meeting by stating that the teacher was concerned about the student's attention (lack of focus on work) and behavior. No mention of reading difficulties was noted. The psychologist was asked to complete an evaluation to help determine special education eligibility due to "other health impairment," and the educational diagnostician began assessing the student for a learning disability.

The child was a few weeks into the second grade when the psychologist began collecting information. Meanwhile the team did not recommend any additional supports to the teacher or the student other than preferential seating for the student and having the teacher check with the student for understanding. As the evaluation began, the first surprise came from the psychologist's data: the student received all E's for behavior, had only one discipline referral, and was described as generally compliant when all teachers were interviewed. In addition, the student was passing all classes except for reading. Two systematic observations of the student revealed that his time on task was 100 percent and that he showed tendencies associated with dyslexia. An analysis of district benchmark data indicated that the child was performing on grade level for all subject areas, with only slight deficits in reading, particularly with fluency.

The end result was that the evaluation did not support a disability condition (behavioral or academic) but found weaknesses in specific reading skills. The student support team was then given specific intervention strategies for working with the student in the general education curriculum.

This process took 45 days under the old pre-referral team model. However, if the team had reviewed existing data thoroughly during its initial referral meeting, a 45-day delay in applying interventions could have been avoided. In this case the team was clearly making decisions based on emotion—teacher frustration and perceived lack of support available through general education means—and not on the data available at the time of the meeting.

pre-referral team
A campus-level team of teachers, counselors, administrators, and support personnel that meets on a regular basis to discuss students who are demonstrating difficulty in the general education setting.

To improve student performance, problem solving needs to be comprehensive in evaluating the curriculum (what is being taught), the instruction (how it is being taught), and the environment (the context in which learning is occurring). *Rule of thumb:* Always let the data drive the decision-making process (figure 4.1). The steps in problem solving for struggling students are as follows:

1. Identify the problem by using available data to determine the skill deficit.
2. Interpret the assessment data to determine which specific areas need to be addressed, according to the student's learning and behavior rates.
3. Develop a plan that specifies interventions, outcome goals, fidelity checks, progress-monitoring methods, and the parties responsible for implementing the plan.

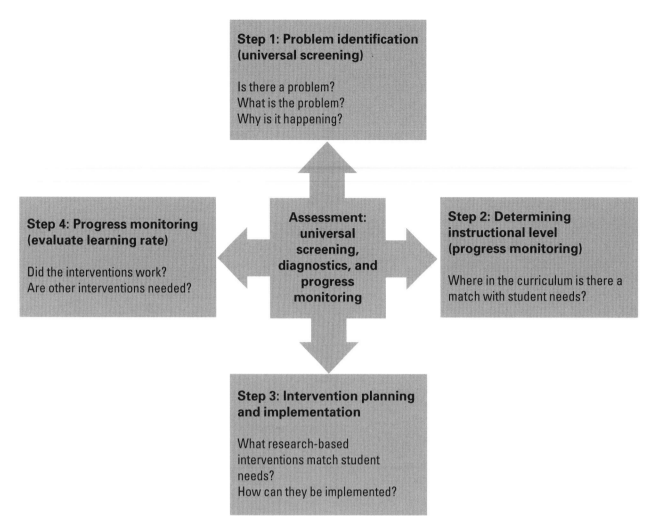

Figure 4.1. The problem-solving method of RtI. Note that each step relies on data gathered through several types of assessments.

4. During implementation, evaluate the effectiveness of interventions by analyzing progress-monitoring data. If students have responded positively, continue the plan; if not, revise the plan and determine if added support is needed.

Problem Solving versus Standard Protocol

standard protocol
Interventions that match a set of research-based practices to students who show predictable patterns of performance.

In RtI, problem solving tailors interventions in order to change student outcomes (performance), while a standard protocol relies on interventions that are standardized. The standard protocol approach is more rigid, but it is not distinctly different from the problem-solving approach outlined above. The problem-solving method uses more flexibility in designing interventions to meet individual student needs, whereas the standard protocol model uses regimented interventions that are not flexible in how they are delivered to the student.

It is recommended that the campus RtI team use *both* approaches. For example, research-based strategies for differentiated instruction and behavioral support tend to be more flexible under Tier 1. On the other hand, the more rigorous interventions of Tiers 2 and 3 may need to be structured and scripted.

When the campus RtI team begins the shift to Tier 2, the recommended focus is on standard protocol interventions. This focus not only will ensure fidelity of implementation but also will help with resource allocation. From a financial and resource-allocation standpoint, it can be very beneficial to the district to select three research-based interventions for each of these areas: reading, math, writing, and behavior. The district can train interventionists on these specific programs and strategies and then use the trained personnel to deliver Tier 2 support. This approach enables the campus administrator to track the fidelity and validity of the interventions more easily.

interventionists Persons trained in specific aspects of academic and behavioral interventions.

Monitoring Academic Progress with Curriculum-Based Measurement

Progress monitoring is the form of assessment used in Tier 2. It is defined as frequent measurement of student progress in a brief, repeatable, reliable, and valid way. Data from progress monitoring enable the campus RtI team to evaluate student growth over time. This type of assessment detects even small advances in skill development and generally uses a measure of fluency (for instance, correct words per minute as a measure of reading fluency). The most typical kind of progress monitoring is often referred to as curriculum-based measurement, or CBM. This research-based assessment method is highly sensitive to the slightest skill development, can be administered quickly over short periods of time, is performed frequently, and can report results in charts and graphs that are easy for teachers, parents, and students to understand.

progress monitoring Frequent measurement of student progress in a brief, repeatable, reliable, and scientifically valid way; usually performed at predetermined intervals to allow for timely modification of instructional design to suit the student's needs.

curriculum-based measurement (CBM) Any set of assessment procedures that use direct observation and recording of a student's performance in a local curriculum to gather information for making instructional decisions.

The purpose of Tier 2 assessment is to determine whether the chosen interventions succeed in advancing learning rates in the student's skill deficit areas. This assessment will guide the team in problem solving for student progress. The recommended schedule for administering CBM assessment in Tier 2 is twice weekly, beginning at the onset of the intervention. The assessment results are charted immediately after the administration, and then preset learning-rate rules

skill deficit A deficiency in a skill that is necessary for learning to occur or for achieving competence in a given area.

probes   In terms of progress monitoring and curriculum-based measurement, refers to brief repeated assessments of an academic skill.

instructional effectiveness   A measure of a teacher's delivery of instruction, based on the positive learning outcomes of students.

delivery of instruction The methods for introducing information to students.

retention rate   A measure of a student's ability to retain and demonstrate a previously learned skill.

(discussed below) are used to determine whether the student is making progress.

CBM is essentially a set of various timed techniques (also referred to as probes) that are elegant in the simplicity of their design, grounded in common sense (it tests what is being taught), and heavily supported by research. CBM assessment consists simply of repeated timed probes using readily available materials (it is cost-efficient), employs standardized administration and scoring techniques (to ensure technical adequacy—that is, consistent and reliable scoring), systematically monitors instructional effectiveness, and requires minimal training (it is easy to do).

The underlying philosophy driving CBM is to begin intervening where the student, especially the struggling learner, is in the curriculum—not where the current curriculum is being taught. Instructional matching is the key to identifying the starting point of the intervention. The campus RtI team must know where to enter into the curriculum for delivery of the instructional intervention and must use the appropriate pace of delivery of the instruction. The assessment information allows the team to match the learner with tasks that are appropriately challenging and that provide a realistic opportunity for success.

Many research studies over the past 30 years have documented the usefulness of CBM. Stanley Deno (1987) defined CBM as any set of measurement procedures that use direct observation and recording of a student's performance in a local curriculum as a basis for gathering information to make instructional decisions. CBM uses fluency measures to provide information for determining the rate of skill acquisition, which is simply identifying the pace of teaching that is best for the student. CBM also gives information regarding retention rate—that is, the ability of the student to retain information that has been taught and to use it in a meaningful way. Typically these rates are useful in identifying what types of interventions may be needed for a student.

The most critical phase of implementing progress monitoring is the training of persons who will be administering, interpreting, and charting the data. Teachers follow a designated procedure and schedule for progress monitoring, administering measures at least twice a week. The assessments themselves are appropriate to the curriculum in which the intervention is occurring (including grade level). Teachers must know how to chart the resulting data. All staff involved must also be trained to analyze the data with regard to instructional effectiveness, so that they can use the information in their decision making. Parents will also need to be informed on how the assessment works. This can be accomplished by providing information through campus newsletters, PTO meetings, and parent trainings.

CBM data link student performance directly to the curriculum and also enhance the academic success and continuous progress of students. The classroom teacher is led by the information to examine the curriculum and decide where entry levels begin for appropriate instruction and intervention. Then the teacher can match meaningful content to the student's instructional level and prior learning. These elements are critical to giving the student an appropriate margin of challenge that allows learning to occur.

An intervention plan based on CBM enables the student to use and build on prior knowledge. Working at an appropriate instructional level allows the student to feel comfortable and competent, which also increases motivation to learn. And the student can adjust the pace of learning to suit himself or herself, because the information provided is not too hard to process.

Lessons Learned: One effective learning strategy is called peer-assisted learning. This technique allows peers to work with struggling learners in areas of needed support. One campus designed its own peer tutoring service. Student tutors enrolled in the program for high school credit and were nominated for the positions by the teachers. After being trained in research-based instructional strategies and CBM, the tutors were able to work effectively with peers as well as with elementary students and were able to document progress using CBM. This particular campus also trained parents to administer CBM probes to aid in the data collection. This worked well, and one result was increased parent participation with the intervention program.

peer-assisted learning
A specific research-based intervention that uses class-wide peer tutoring techniques developed by Doug and Lynn Fuchs.

Measurement tools used in CBM involve specific skills in the areas of reading, math, spelling, and writing. The oral reading probes are given individually to students in a quiet location. Reading probes generally allow 1 to 2 minutes for administration. The reading skill to be assessed is identified, and a probe for the skill is randomly chosen, such as phoneme segmentation. The student sits opposite the examiner, who has a numbered copy of the probe to score and follows a script to give directions. The student then begins to read aloud until the examiner says, "Stop." The examiner times the oral reading with a stopwatch. There are specific scoring criteria. A fluency rate (accuracy and speed) is determined from the score. The student is given three probes during the assessment. The examiner chooses the median (middle) score of the three probes and then asks the student to plot the score on a graph. By plotting the progress-monitoring chart, the student becomes part of the problem-solving process.

Many struggling learners do not have good learning habits or strategies, because they are so busy struggling in a curriculum that is not on their instructional level. When asked to plot the CBM scores within his or her instructional level, the student then can problem-solve aloud with the teacher about strategies that may be working or not working. This increases the student's motivation significantly.

positive reinforcement
The process of associating a desired behavior with a desired consequence, which then increases the probability that the behavior will be repeated.

Lessons Learned: Steven was a second-grade student exhibiting both reading difficulties and behavior problems (mostly due to avoidance of reading tasks). He was reinforced in reading when he participated in graphing his progress. At the beginning of the intervention, Steven often responded by throwing his papers on the floor and refusing to participate. After approximately 7 weeks of intervention and positive reinforcement, Steven was graphing his charts and showing an increased interest in his reading program. One day when he was having difficulty because he had reached a plateau in his progress, he talked with the school psychologist and his teacher about how disappointed he was that his "dots on the chart" were not moving. This was significant because in the past he did not problem-solve; instead he disrupted. Steven then discussed what he felt was missing from his intervention (his mother was working late and not implementing the flash card practice at home). The school psychologist and the teacher immediately contacted Steven's mother and arranged for a high school tutor to work with Steven to take the pressure off his mother and to get Steven back on track with his intervention. The RtI team did not "admire the problem" by allowing the mother's unavailability to become an excuse for the lack of intervention success. Instead the team focused on his need and problem-solved to find a way to meet the need creatively and effectively. Once the tutor began working with Steven, progress in his learning rates, as measured through CBM, resumed.

In math, students are asked to answer as many items possible in 2 to 6 minutes on single-skill or multiple-skill computation probes that are designed to assess fluency of basic skills. On probes that measure concepts and applications of higher-order math skills, the time limits are 6 to 8 minutes. Math CBM probes can be given individually, to a small group of students, or to the whole class. The probes are scored immediately, and the student enters the score onto a graph. Fuchs and colleagues (2006) have identified expected learning-rate norms for mathematics.

In the area of written language, the student is given a lined composition sheet with a story starter sentence. The student is instructed to think for 1 minute about what he or she is going to write, and then is given 3 minutes to write the story. The story is scored for accuracy, grammar, sentence structure, and punctuation. The score is given to the student, who charts it on a graph.

Graphing of the data is done by plotting the number of correct words, letters, or problems on the vertical axis of the chart by the date of probe on the horizontal axis. The first CBM scores to be collected are called the baseline data points.

Table 4.1. The first-grade oral reading fluency standard reported by Tindal, Hasbrouck, and Jones (2005)

Percentile	Fall WCPM★	Winter WCPM	Spring WCPM	Average Weekly Improvement (Learning Rate)
90	—	81	111	1.9
75	—	47	82	2.2
50	—	23	53	1.9
25	—	12	28	1.0
10	—	6	15	0.6

★WCPM = words correct per minute.

Baseline data points indicate where the student's instructional level is within the curriculum before the intervention begins. The baseline data points (3 probes) are plotted on the graph, and the median (middle) score is chosen as the beginning point of measurement for progress. This median point is then marked with an X and becomes the basis for all comparisons to determine whether the student is making progress from an intensified intervention.

Next, the team meets to decide on what the student's outcome goal (predicted skill level) will be, based on the intervention. Guidelines have been developed for expected learning rates (pace of skill acquisition). One such published set of reading norms for first through eighth grades can be found in research reported by Tindal, Hasbrouck, and Jones (2005). The norms include averages of expected words correct per minute (WCPM) at the start of the school year, as well as the expected average weekly gains when students are given instruction. This is important because decisions regarding intervention will be based not only on overall fluency scores but also on expected gains when instruction matches student needs. A norm table such as one from Tindal, Hasbrouck, and Jones is used to predict learning goals (table 4.1).

The RtI team must determine the student's intervention outcome goal by first selecting a target date to review the progress monitoring. Once that date is determined (typically 9 to 12 weeks within Tier 2), the team multiplies the number of weeks of intervention by the improvement rate selected from published norms for reading, writing, written language, and spelling. That number is added to the baseline rate to obtain the outcome goal.

> *Example:* Emily is a fourth grader who read 50 words correctly at baseline in a second-grade reading passage. A reasonable weekly improve-

baseline data point An initial score that indicates a student's skill level before intervention; serves as the starting point in curriculum-based measurement of the student's response to the intervention.

outcome goal The targeted goal of an intervention plan.

Progress-Monitoring Graph for Reading

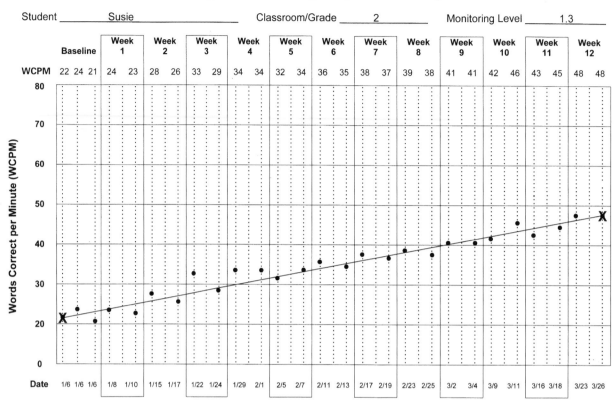

Figure 4.2. Example of a progress-monitoring graph. Solid circles indicate the student's median score of words correct per minute (WCPM) for each date of CBM administration. The X at the lower left marks the student's starting data point, and the X at the right marks the outcome goal on the last administration day. The straight line between the Xs is called the aimline. This student's data indicate that her progress is appropriate to the outcome goals defined in the aimline. The team's decision to continue the current intervention is appropriate. *Source:* Adapted from Intervention Central (www.interventioncentral.org).

ment rate for her would be 1 word correct per minute gain per week. The intervention team determined that the period of intervention was going to be 10 weeks.

10 weeks X 1 word gained per week = 10 words gained

50 words correct + 10 words gained = 60 words correct (outcome goal)

Once the team establishes the baseline and the outcome goal, the next step is to graph the student performance.

Districts can design their own graphs, or many of the resources mentioned above also provide scoring graphs. To set up a progress-monitoring graph, label the horizontal axis with the dates of the CBM administration (typically by weeks of intervention) and the vertical axis with the CBM skill measure, such as words correct per minute in multiples of 5 or 10 (for a sample graph for a 12-week monitoring period, see figure 4.2). The graph should be labeled with the student's name and the skill area to be measured. The first points to be recorded on the graph are the student's baseline data. Typically the student's three baseline data points are recorded, with the median score (middle) marked with an X to denote starting data point. Next, place an X on the graph at the intersection of the final day of intervention on the horizontal axis and the outcome goal on the vertical axis. Then draw a line connecting the baseline data point to the outcome goal. This line represents the aimline for judging progress. The progress monitoring continues by plotting the median score for each administration on the graph.

The RtI team uses a set of decision rules for determining whether changes are needed in the student's intervention program. The research suggests using a data-point decision rule (Wright 2006). This rule should be applied after approximately 6 data points have been charted (not counting the baseline data points). The basic data-point decision rule is this: If three points are below the aimline, change the intervention. If three data points are above the aimline, adjust the aimline. And if the consecutive data points are falling within expected rates of growth, continue with the current program.

aimline A visual representation (line) on a progress-monitoring graph that connects the baseline data point to the outcome goal.

data-point decision rule A means of interpreting curriculum-based measurement data (points on a graph) in order to make decisions about a student's intervention plan.

Lessons Learned: John was a second-grade student who was referred for Tier 2 intervention. His teacher reported he was reading within the second half of the first-grade reading book (WCPM = 43). The team knew that in order for John to be progressing, he needed to be improving his reading fluency into a second-grade reader. The team determined that he should be reading 60 WCPM in the first-grade reader before introducing him to instruction on a second-grade level. The average expected learning rate increase for a first-grade reader was 2 WCPM, so the team decided that at the end of the 6-week intervention period John would need to show a gain of 12 WCPM to demonstrate intervention success.

The team added the 12-word expected improvement to John's baseline rate of 43 WCPM to arrive at an outcome goal of 55 WCPM by the end of week 6. If John demonstrated this rate at the end of the intervention period, the data would support the effectiveness of the intervention. The team's next step was to mark the baseline data point on the graph with an X, along with another X at the intersection of week 6 on the horizontal axis and 55 WCPM on the vertical axis.

Now the team was ready to begin John's intervention and progress monitoring. Each week, John would be given CBM probes (preferably 2 probes per week), and the median scores of the probes would be plotted on the graph. The data-point decision rule would be applied to the charted points to determine whether a change in the intervention was needed.

An important resource for helping a school district determine which CBM tool will meet its particular needs is the National Center on Student Progress Monitoring's "Tools Chart," found in the Tools section of the center's website (www.studentprogress.org). All of the tools on the chart have been reviewed by a committee and evaluated using rigorous criteria for easy comparison. If you are interested in a specific CBM tool, you can also click on its name for vendor information regarding features, cost, and other details. Districts may also wish to use the wealth of information provided at Intervention Central (www.interventioncentral.org) for developing CBM in reading, writing, and math.

Commercially developed CBM assessments that are available for districts to use include these:

- AIMSweb (www.aimsweb.com)
- DIBELS (Dynamic Indicators of Basic Early Literacy Skills; dibels .uoregon.edu)
- STEEP (www.isteep.com)

The National Research Center on Learning Disabilities has identified valuable resources for principals and teachers that support progress monitoring (Johnson et al. 2006). The center recommends the following resources for district personnel:

- Edcheckup (www.edcheckup.com)
- EdProgress (www.edprogress.com)
- McGraw-Hill Digital Learning (www.mhdigitallearning.com)
- Minnesota Reading Excellence Act (Stanley Deno; cehd.umn.edu/ Pubs/ResearchWorks/CBM.html)
- Monitoring Basic Skills Progress (MBSP) (Fuchs; www.proedinc.com)
- Read Naturally (www.readnaturally.com)

Functional Behavioral Assessment

emotional disturbance eligibility Qualification of a student as eligible to receive special supports to counteract a chronic behavior or emotional condition that adversely affects his or her educational performance.

Tier 2 behavioral assessment focuses on systematic data collection and interpretation for use in designing behavior supports. It is important to note that IDEA 2004 did not change the criteria for emotional disturbance eligibility. The data collected in Tier 2 are used to verify that a problem exists by objectively defining the behavior, to prioritize behavioral concerns, and then to specify realistic and achievable criteria for success.

The philosophy behind functional behavioral assessment allows the staff to understand the context in which a problem behavior is occurring. Functional behavioral assessment moves staff away from a reactive, consequence-based approach toward the identification and teaching of appropriate alternate behaviors. The purpose of functional behavior assessment is to identify important functional relationships of a set of targeted behaviors for a particular student. Functional behavioral assessment data can also identify multiple underlying causes that contribute to the expression of the problem behavior.

Conducting a functional behavioral assessment results in five primary outcomes:

1. Operational description of the problem behavior
2. Identification of events, times, and situations that predict when a problem behavior occurs across a range of typical daily routines
3. Identification of the functions and consequences of the problem behavior
4. Creation of a hypothesis statement
5. Design of interventions using replacement behaviors, teaching strategies, environmental changes, and progress monitoring

The basics principles of functional behavioral assessment are that behavior is learned; behavior serves a communicative function; information gathered is used to determine interventions, which include teaching the desired alternate behaviors; and interventions are aligned with the functions of the behavior.

The purpose of initial data collection is to identify the function of the behaviors by analyzing antecedent events (events that trigger the problem behavior) and consequences (events that support the continuation of the problem behavior). For example, students often engage in behaviors to obtain things they want or to escape or avoid things they find difficult or do not like.

Data sources for functional behavioral assessment include a review of student records:

- Discipline referrals
- Behavior incidents
- Classroom and school-wide observations
- Teacher interviews
- Student self-assessments
- Attendance records
- Parent interview

Additional data are collected to help the RtI team objectively define the problem behavior in the context of the settings in which it occurs and the intensity, fre-

functional behavioral assessment A collection of information about events that predict and maintain a student's problem behavior; used to construct a behavior action plan.

problem behavior Behavior that has been identified as impeding the learning of the student or of others in the student's environment.

antecedent event An event that triggers a problem behavior.

consequence What happens immediately after a behavior occurs.

quency, and duration of the behavior. The data should document any previous interventions attempted and their outcomes, as well as the impact the negative behavior has on student learning and classroom disruptions. The assessment should not focus only on negative behaviors, however. It should also identify the student's academic and behavioral strengths. (See the RtI Documentation of Student Behavior form on pages 79–80.

The first step of the functional behavioral assessment is to operationally define the behavior of concern in measurable terms. This means that the behavior should be described in such a way that anyone who reads the description clearly understands what the behavior looks like. For instance "off task" is not an operational definition. However, "stares down at feet," "taps pencil on desk," and "touches peers' papers" are good examples of operational definitions of behavior.

Step two is to collect data specific to the identified problem behavior. The data should be collected across settings and people. It should also identify instruction, curriculum, and environmental factors associated with the problem behavior. Another helpful piece of data is called a setting event—an event that is removed in time from the occurrence of the problem behavior but is related to it. Setting events may include medications, sleep cycles, eating routines and diet, daily schedules, staffing patterns and interactions, academic tasks, and social demands.

Next, the function of the behavior is identified. Most often the function is to get something or to avoid something. However, research indicates that functions of behavior will vary if the student has underlying emotional regulation problems, increasing the likelihood that the function is more than just to escape or obtain something. Areas to consider when conducting a functional behavioral assessment on a student suspected of underlying emotional conditions may include emotional reactivity due to depression, anger, or anxiety; distorted thought patterns; reinforcement due to environmental triggers; modeling of inappropriate behaviors; family issues; developmental disabilities; functional communication needs; and the educational setting.

It is not possible for the RtI team to define the function of a problem behavior without understanding the context in which the behavior occurs. The data provided by Tier 1 documentation are very helpful in this stage. Also, the problem behavior may have more than one function attached to it.

Once the RtI team identifies the behavior's function, the next step is to generate a hypothesis statement. This statement is related to the defined function of the problem behavior and includes the behavior and the conditions under which it occurs.

operational definition
A description of behaviors that are observable and measurable.

setting event   An event that is removed in time from the occurrence of a problem behavior but is related to it.

disordered thoughts
Abnormal thoughts associated with emotional conditions.

environmental triggers
Events or situations in the student's environment that bring about a behavioral response.

functional communication   The use of language in a meaningful and understandable way.

hypothesis statement
In the functional behavioral assessment, the statement that identifies the function that maintains a student's problem behavior (what the student gets out of the behavior).

Lessons Learned: The RtI team met to discuss George's problem behavior as documented by his teacher. The team reviewed all data and generated the following hypothesis statement:

> When George has spent the weekend at his noncustodial parent's house and he is presented an independent task without visual cues or prompts on the Monday morning after the visit, he demonstrates passive noncompliance by placing his head down on his desk to avoid completing the task.

The team's hypothesis statement can be broken into the following elements:

Setting event: George spends the weekend at his noncustodial parent's house

Antecedent event (trigger): He is presented with an independent task without visual cues or prompts on the Monday morning after the visit

Behavior: He demonstrates passive noncompliance (head down on desk)

Function: To avoid completing the task

passive noncompliance
The failure of a student to perform a teacher's request, often by acting as if he or she did not hear it.

The fifth step in functional behavioral assessment begins with designing the intervention. The RtI team generates a list of possible alternate behaviors. In order for the intervention to be effective, the alternate behaviors must achieve the same function that the problem behavior does. For example, if the problem behavior's function is to avoid a task, then the alternate behavior must also provide the opportunity to avoid the task.

Lessons Learned: Susan was a third-grade student who consistently threw her math worksheets (double-digit subtraction with regrouping) on the floor when her teacher gave her the task. Assessment information indicated that Susan was working on her instructional level; however, she needed more time than most students to complete tasks. Susan's worksheets were modified by giving her 5 problems to complete at a time instead of 20 problems per worksheet. She was placed on a positive behavior support system that required her to complete the 5 problems without throwing the paper on the floor. She would then earn the opportunity to place an X over one problem on the next worksheet (effectively allowing her to earn the

positive behavior support system
A systematic approach that clearly establishes behavioral expectations and uses reinforcement when the student demonstrates appropriate behaviors.

right to avoid one problem). This system worked very well for Susan, and within 3 weeks she was no longer demonstrating the avoidant behavior of throwing her worksheets on the floor.

When designing interventions to recommend based on the functional behavioral assessment data, the RtI team should focus on three areas:

> *Instruction:* Identify current instructional levels, and match academic interventions to instructional needs.
> *Behavior:* Identify positive behavior support plans and strategies to train and shape appropriate behaviors.
> *Environment:* Modify the environment to increase the likelihood of positive learning and behavior outcomes.

The following questions may help focus the recommendations on these three areas:

> What are the curriculum demands and the student's current skill level?
> What types of specific interventions would lead to an increase in the alternate behaviors?
> What type of environment would lead to a decrease in the inappropriate behavior?

Finally, the RtI team needs to decide on appropriate data collection techniques for progress monitoring of behavioral interventions. The most common type of direct assessment of behavior involves systematic observations.

A skilled and trained observer must observe the behavior in natural settings, classify the behavior objectively as it occurs, ensure the reliability of the observation, and convert the information to quantify occurrences of the behavior. According to Sattler (2002), skilled observers are trained to distinguish behaviors in operationally defined terms. They sustain attention during the observation and focus on details in the environment. Skilled observers are able to document behaviors efficiently and are able to summarize data in succinct terms. (See the RtI Classroom Observation Form on page 56, for example.)

The primary objective of using direct observations is to keep the data collection simple. RtI team members need to be trained on how to select times for conducting observations—such as choosing an activity that is compatible with the occurrence of the target problem behavior, selecting a variety of times and settings for observation, and choosing times when the student is likely to demonstrate a variety of behaviors. Training includes helping observers focus on specific

direct observations
Systematic, structured observations that use well-designed observation record forms.

details when special circumstances occur during the observation such as a fire drill, a substitute teacher, or peer misbehavior.

The following are examples of questions that can be asked during a direct observation in the classroom:

> Does the student engage in the target problem behavior with one teacher but not another?
>
> Does the target behavior occur at school but not at home?
>
> Does the target behavior occur in the morning but not in the afternoon?

Several methods can be used to record direct observations:

> *Anecdotal recording:* Maintaining a simple running record and account of what is happening in the environment. This account can be handwritten, keyed in on a computer, audio-taped, or videotaped.
>
> *Interval recording:* Dividing observations into brief segments (15–30 minutes). The observer tallies the presence or absence of the defined target problem behavior during the discrete time period.
>
> *Event recording:* Recording each instance of the target problem behavior as it occurs throughout an observation period.
>
> *ABC:* Documenting <u>a</u>ntecedent event (what happens before), <u>b</u>ehavior (occurrence of the target problem behavior), and <u>c</u>onsequence (what immediately happens after the behavior).

In addition to collecting data through direct observation, the RtI team needs to review records to identify any factors that may contribute to the occurrence of the problem behavior, such as issues at home, in the community, or at school, as well as disabilities. Poverty and language barriers may be contributing factors. Interactions between parent and child and other social interactions may also affect behavior progress.

Measurement should focus on the reduction of the targeted problem behavior as well as the occurrence of the taught alternate behavior. Fidelity of implementation of the positive behavior support system is essential for behavior change. Campus staff must also understand that behavior change takes time, and they should not rush to judgment within a brief period of time (i.e., less than 6 weeks).

Strategic Interventions: Academic

Strategic interventions at Tier 2 are intended as supplements within the general education classroom. This level of intervention is designed for students who have not made progress within the curriculum and instructional strategies provided in Tier 1. Students who are referred to Tier 2 interventions also continue to receive Tier 1 supports and curriculum. The Tier 2 interventions are delivered in groups of 2 to 4 students. The RtI team arranges for the intervention to occur 3 or 4 times per week (30–45 minutes per session). The interventions are implemented by trained and supervised staff, not by the general education teacher. Typical duration of interventions at this stage is 9 to 12 weeks (repeated as needed).

Tier 2 interventions are designed with individualized goals for each identified struggling learner. The interventions are research-based, and progress monitoring occurs twice weekly during the intervention phase.

The most important aspect of selecting interventions at Tier 2 is that they be aligned with the data collected in Tier 1. The RtI team should analyze the student's data to determine whether a deficit is skill-based or performance-based. The intervention plan must determine and chart the outcome goals that have been defined specific to the student's academic skill deficit, and it should include who will intervene, when the intervention will occur, and what resources are needed for success.

Interventions must also meet research-based standards as defined in NCLB and IDEA 2004 (refer to the discussion of these standards in Chapter 3, "Universal Academic Interventions"). Some helpful websites review intervention resources:

skill deficit A deficiency in a skill that is necessary for learning to occur or for competence in a given area.

performance deficit An inability to demonstrate a skill that has been learned.

- Best Evidence Encyclopedia (www.bestevidence.org)
- Florida Center for Reading Research (www.fcrr.org)
- National Research Center on Learning Disabilities (www.nrcld.org)
- Reading Rockets (www.readingrockets.org)
- What Works Clearinghouse (ies.ed.gov/ncee/wwc/)

Additional research-based Tier 2 interventions include, but are not limited to, the following:

Reading
- Corrective Reading (SRA/McGraw Hill; www.sraonline.com)
- Daisy Quest (Erickson; DaisyQuest@comcast.net)
- Fast ForWord (Tallal; www.scilearn.com)

- Kaplan SpellRead (Kaplan; www.kaplank12.com)
- Open Court (SRA/McGraw Hill; www.sraonline.com)
- Peer-Assisted Learning Strategies (PALS) (Vanderbilt Kennedy Center for Research on Human Development; kc.vanderbilt.edu/pals)
- Plato Learning (www.plato.com)
- Read 180 (Scholastic; teacher.scholastic.com/products/read180/)
- Reading Recovery (Marie Clay; www.readingrecovery.org)
- Rigby Literacy (rigby.harcourtachieve.com)
- Stepping Stones to Literacy (Sopris West; www.spriswest.com)
- Voyager Expanded Learning—Passport (www.voyagerlearning.com)

Writing
- Write Well (Sopris West; www.spriswest.com)

Mathematics—elementary
- Everyday Mathematics (SRA/McGraw Hill; www.wrightgroup.com)

Mathematics—middle school
- Connected Mathematics (Pearson Prentice Hall; connectedmath.msu.edu)
- I CAN Learn Pre-Algebra and Algebra (JRL Enterprises; www.icanlearn.com)
- Mathletics (www.mathletics.com.au)
- Neufeld math curriculum (www.neufeldmath.com)
- Saxon Middle Grades Math (Saxon; saxonpublishers.harcourt achieve.com)
- Transition Mathematics (USSMP; www.phschool.com/atschool/ucsmp/)

Strategic Interventions: Behavioral

Even when solid positive behavior support systems are in place on a school-wide basis, some students (15 to 20 percent) will need additional strategic interventions that are individualized to their needs. Tier 2 behavioral interventions are applied more often, are administered individually or within a small group (2 to 4 students), and are frequently monitored. (See the RtI Behavior Action Plan form on page 81.) Although individual students will need strategic interventions for problem behaviors, it is important to note that *positive* behavior support interventions are not a specific curriculum nor are they limited to a certain group of students.

Each of the strategic behavioral interventions at Tier 2 has the following characteristics:

- The intervention is readily available.
- It is implemented by assigned staff from the RtI team.
- It is consistent with the school-wide positive support plan.
- It is driven by functional behavioral assessment data.

Tier 2 strategic interventions should improve the structure of the student's environment by tailoring it to the student's individual needs, and they should provide for frequent feedback and increased opportunities for success. Interventions should be designed to be implemented across all settings (are easy to do in classes and common areas such as the cafeteria, halls, and playground), to link the behavior supports to academic supports, to include opportunities for positive reinforcement, and to teach self-management skills.

A wide variety of interventions can be incorporated in a strategic behavior action plan at Tier 2. Education (training and instruction), skill building, self-monitoring, and reinforcement can be combined to devise effective interventions, such as the following, to address particular problems.

Stress inoculation: Teachers train students to use coping skills when they are frustrated with social or learning situations. The students are taught to focus on needed skills, rehearsing them and then applying them in the school or home setting.

Proactive intervention and insight training: Students learn to recognize behaviors that cause distress in their environment, and then they problem-solve ways to modify or change the behavior. This type of training is very helpful for students who experience behavioral issues related to depression and anxiety.

Anger management training: Students learn strategies to help themselves reduce emotional and phyical responses to stressful triggers of anger. Anger management training also teaches students to use thinking rehearsal strategies to promote problem solving for dealing with frustration and stressful events.

Parent training: Parents are given helpful tips for managing their children's behavior at home. This strategy is proactive, focusing on suggestions to help prevent the problem behavior in the first place.

Behavior contracting: A contract is developed with the student that relates to work completion or designates appropriate behaviors within the classroom.

Social skills training: Training focuses on the skills needed for successful social interactions, such as entering into a conversation or asking for help.

Precision command requests: Requests are delivered by using a series of non-emotional commands in a consistent manner that allows the adult to maintain control of the situation. This technique is very helpful with students who demonstrate high levels of noncompliance.

Behavioral momentum: The student is asked to do two or three things he or she is likely to do (preferred activities), in order to create a positive behavior flow before a request is made for a behavior that the student is less likely to do.

Behavior rehearsal: The student is taught the desired behavior and then is given opportunities to rehearse it in the natural classroom setting.

Peer-initialed modeling: The student's peers are taught how to demonstrate specific behaviors that are required to complete a desired task. The peers then serve as role models for the student. While they all are completing the desired activity, the teacher gives the student corrective feedback paired with positive reinforcement to promote behavioral and academic skill acquisition.

Group contingency system: In this reinforcement strategy, the whole group (the class) must meet a desired outcome or standard before a positive reinforcement is given.

Reinforcement token economy system: This positive behavior support strategy is proactive by encouraging good behaviors with incentives. When students demonstrate a desired behavior, they earn a token, which can be saved and redeemed later for a reinforcer (such as extra time on the computer, a homework pass, or lunch with a favored teacher).

Excellent resources for developing behavioral intervention strategies are available, including the following:

- Intervention Central (www.interventioncentral.org)
- Positive Behavioral Interventions and Supports (PBIS; www.pbis.org)
- Project Achieve (www.projectachieve.info)
- Safe and Civil Schools (www.safeandcivilschools.com)

To summarize, these are the keys to developing a good behavior action plan:

1. Modify events before the problem behavior occurs (setting events, antecedent events).
2. Teach the student the new alternate behavior that is expected to replace the problem behavior.
3. Increase and improve the positive consequences the student receives for demonstrating the positive alternate behavior.
4. Strengthen the consequences for demonstrating the problem behavior.
5. Continuously evaluate the plan using identified behavior recording techniques.

Lessons Learned: The most common problems arising from the implementation of Tier 2 academic and behavioral strategic interventions have involved districts and campuses that did not define cutoff scores or establish data-point decision rules to monitor student progress. In addition, when interventions were not clearly defined or implemented with fidelity at Tier 2, campuses experienced difficulties related to the problem-solving process because the campus RtI teams were reluctant to conduct fidelity checks. Some of the most critical problems occurred when RtI teams did not effectively document their intervention plans or progress monitoring.

To avoid these problems, follow the procedural guidelines in this book for setting up the RtI process, and then evaluate the consistency with which documentation, fidelity checks, and corrective feedback are used by the campus RtI team. When there is consistency in delivering the Tier 2 process, extraordinary progress can be made with even the simplest academic and behavioral interventions.

RtI Documentation of Student Behavior

Name __Harry H.__   DOB __4/0/97__
Grade __4__   Teacher(s) __S. Reaves, P. Smith__
Team Member __Counselor__   School _____
Team Member __LSSP__
Team Member __Teacher(s)__

Purpose
(Why is the team gathering the behavior data?)

Harry is demonstrating difficulty with sustaining attention during teacher-led instruction. He is also described as "immature," which is impacting social skills.

Methods of Data Collection
(Check all that apply.)

✓ Comprehensive record review   _____ Parent interview
✓ Teacher interview   _____ Student interview
_____ ABC Chart   ✓ Structured observations
_____ Anecdotal records   ✓ Academic skills level
✓ Behavior action plan
_____ Other:

Background Information
(Include behavior data—teacher documentation, office referrals, disciplinary actions, critical incidents—and information about previous interventions.)

Mrs. Reaves documented using a time-on-task analysis; off-task behaviors at 65% during teacher-led instruction. Teachers report social difficulties during lunch and recess due to attention-seeking behaviors.

Student Characteristics and Strengths — No formal discipline referrals.
(Identify special talents, preferred activities, academic skills, etc.)

Harry has good attendance, is highly motivated to learn, and has above-average ability in science and math.

Description of Behavior(s)
(Include frequency, duration, and intensity)

① According to teacher documentation using behavior charts, George demonstrates difficulty with social interactions daily during lunch and recess (Average of crying indicates 3 times per week in recess; Average teasing of female peers - 2 incidents per daily lunch period.)

② Measured time off-task is 65% during class instruction.

Page 1 of 2

Antecedents/Patterns of Identified Behavior(s)
(What occurs prior to the behavior? Identify time of day, setting, academic/nonacademic activity, etc.)

Off-task antecedent is verbal instructions during non-preferred academic activity (reading, Social Studies)

Teasing and name calling occurs daily during lunch.

Consequences (Positive or Negative) That May Influence Behavior(s)
(What occurs after the behavior? Identify teacher responses, peer responses, other.)

Off-task consequence is avoidance of task.

Teasing/name calling consequence is immediate peer attention.

Additional Factors That May Have an Impact on Behavior(s)
(Include information such as cultural, familial, and environmental factors.)

Harry has demonstrated difficulty when in large groups to sustain attention.

Possible Function(s) of Behavior(s)
(What might the student obtain, escape, or attempt to communicate through the behavior?)

Off-task function is to escape non-preferred task.

Teasing/name calling function is to obtain peer attention.

Replacement Behavior(s)
(What behaviors will meet the behavioral function and can be addressed and promoted through the behavior action plan?)

Replacement off-task behavior is academic engagement and replacemtent Teasing/name calling is appropriate initiation into peer interactions.

Intervention Recommendations

Continued use of Behavior Action Plan with daily monitoring of frequency of targeted behaviors.

RtI Behavior Action Plan

Name: _____ Grade: _____ School: _____ Date: _____

Goal (based on target behaviors and replacement behaviors identified in Functional Behavioral Assessment)

_____

This intervention plan will address the following:

____ Antecedents ____ Behavioral Skill Deficits ____ Academic Skill Deficits ____ Positive Reinforcement ____ Consequences

____ Crisis Intervention ____ Environmental Changes ____ Other

The following research-based interventions and strategies will address this function: _____

Specific Interventions and Strategies	Person(s) Responsible	Revisions (Include date)

Identify dates for evaluation of student's progress toward goal:

Behavior to be measured	Baseline Data (Quantitative)	Goal	Review Date & Behavioral Data	Review Date & Behavioral Data	Review Date & Behavioral Data	Review Date & Behavioral Data	Review Date & Behavioral Data	Review Date & Behavioral Data

Chapter 5

Tier 3 and Beyond

Intensifying Interventions for Students Who Are Still Struggling

Section 504 committee
A school-based team that meets to discuss the needs of a student with a disability condition and how the condition affects learning. (Section 504 is a federal law that prohibits discrimination against individuals with disabilities.)

Tier 3 in the RtI process is designed for students who have significant difficulties making progress, despite receiving Tier 1 and Tier 2 interventions. Tier 3 provides the most intensive and individualized interventions to the student. The main difference between this tier and Tier 2 is that Tier 3 interventions are more frequent and of longer duration, and either the group size is reduced or the student receives the intervention individually.

As the RtI team collaborates with teachers and parents to provide strategic interventions for students within Tier 2, progress monitoring drives their decision making. The campus RtI team monitors the student progress data for the amount of time the district guidelines recommend—usually 9 to 12 weeks. At the designated time—9 weeks, for example—the RtI team meets, reviews progress, and then uses its preset decision rules to decide whether (a) to continue with Tier 2 interventions for another 9 weeks because the student is demonstrating progress, (b) to return the student to Tier 1 because he or she has made significant gains, or (c) to refer the student for Tier 3 interventions. Usually about 5 percent of the students on a campus advance to Tier 3.

It is important to note that shifting into Tier 3 does not automatically generate a referral for Section 504 committee support or for special education eligibility. Rather, Tier 3 signals intensifying the interventions while monitoring the student's progress to determine whether resources need to be adjusted. If a student's learning rates have not accelerated after the predetermined amount of time (9 to 12 weeks), then the RtI team considers whether the student needs additional services, such as special education.

Monitoring Academic and Behavioral Progress

Assessments of learning and behavior at Tier 3 continue as designed in Tier 2, using CBM and behavior charting to monitor progress. However, the RtI team may increase the progress monitoring to 3 times per week, from the 2 times per week that occurred within Tier 2.

Behavioral assessment may include updating the functional behavioral assessment that occurred within Tier 2. After analyzing the student's behavior charts, the RtI team may decide that the behavior action plan needs to be modified or that additional supports for behavioral or social skills are needed.

More Intensive and Individualized Interventions

The interventions at Tier 3 may be the same standard protocol program that was being used in Tier 2. The difference is in the intensity of the interventions. For instance, if the student was receiving reading interventions through the Voyager Passport reading program 3 times a week for 30 minutes each in a group of 4 students, in Tier 3 the student would receive the intervention 5 times a week for 1 hour per session, individually or with no more than 2 other students.

Also important to note is that the student in Tier 3 continues with Tier 1 interventions. This means that the student remains in the general education classroom for initial instruction with a differentiated approach (Tier 1), and the student receives the Tier 3 interventions at a designated time during the day.

The most important administrative support needed at this level is the flexible scheduling of general education and intervention support staff, in order to accommodate the intensive interventions of Tier 3. Remember that only about 5 percent of the student population on the campus will fall within Tier 3. Therefore the number of students needing this level of intervention will not overwhelm the RtI team and campus staff.

The district RtI team may want to add another intervention at Tier 3, in addition to using intensified Tier 2 interventions. To do this, it is recommended that the district team develop a standard protocol of interventions from which the campus teams can choose (for details, see "Problem Solving versus Standard Protocol" in Chapter 4). Like all RtI interventions, those in the protocols are identified according to research-based standards. Having a protocol helps streamline training and resource allocation. and it aids in the fidelity of implementation. For these reasons, using a standard protocol approach for selecting targeted interventions at Tier 3 makes sense.

Lessons Learned: One school district developed a standard protocol that specified that Tier 2 students could receive the following intervention programs for reading: Read 180, Plato Reading, and Great Leaps. The district also identified one Tier 3 reading intervention: Voyager Passport. The district then trained interventionists and select staff on each campus on how to implement these interventions. After the first year of piloting the RtI process, the district analyzed data from two pilot campuses. The data revealed that on each campus 25 children received the Tier 2 reading interventions and 7 children on each campus additionally received the Tier 3 intervention. Of the 14 children who received the Tier 3 intervention, 3 did not demonstrate sufficient progress and were referred for special education assessment. Interestingly all but one of the 50 children who received these interventions passed the state assessment in reading.

Three Tiers or Four Tiers?

There has sometimes been confusion regarding how special education and Section 504 services fit into the RtI model. Think of these services as being on the continuum of service delivery. If a student continues to show a significant lack of progress in learning rate despite all of the Tier 2 and 3 interventions—and the fidelity of the intervention plan has been documented—then that evidence would indicate that referral for additional services needs to be considered.

There has also been much confusion as to where special services are located on the RtI continuum of service delivery. Remember that moving a student into Tier 3 does not automatically generate a referral for a multidisciplinary assessment. To avoid any confusion, some districts follow a four-tier RtI model in which Tier 4 is identified as special education.

RtI and Special Education Identification

Response to Intervention is not designed to be a pre-referral process. It is not a model in which students must "fail" before interventions begin. Instead, it is a proactive, positive approach for supporting all learners, particularly those who are struggling. RtI meets the students where they are within the curriculum and positively affects their learning rates. To accomplish this, RtI uses research-based interventions that have known positive effects on struggling students. Research has shown that when students are engaged in the curriculum on their instructional level, approximately 95 percent of them will respond positively without the need for Tier 3 interventions.

Although the RtI process may take longer to refer students for special education assessment than the traditional pre-referral approach does, the students are already receiving intensive individualized instruction and interventions beginning at Tier 2. Think in terms of the struggling learner at Tier 3. If this student is referred for special education and qualifies for it, naturally the goals and objectives of the individualized education plan (IEP) will closely match what is already occurring on the RtI team's intervention plan (although the intensity and allocation of services will change). Additionally, students who receive special education as their Tier 3 intervention must also continue receiving Tier 1 supports. Therefore these students remain in the general education class for differentiated instruction in their skill deficit areas and then receive their Tier 3 special education support at another time. It is important for parents and educators to understand that even if a student is identified with a special education eligibility for a learning disability (LD) or a problem behavior, the general education classroom teacher remains the teacher of record, and the special education staff (using Tier 3 interventions outlined on the IEP) support the general education staff in achieving positive outcomes for the student.

The movement toward an RtI process for identification of learning disabilities occurred because research showed that many children were incorrectly identified as having a learning disability when in fact they had not received strong instruction. The idea behind the RtI process is simple: if the students are given access to the research-based instructional practices that are proven to be effective for struggling learners, then the learning rates for the students will show positive outcomes without the need of a labeling system.

In order for an LD identification process to be solid within a district that is using RtI, the staff will need training in areas such as these:

- Interpretation of universal screening
- Collection and interpretation of progress-monitoring data (CBM)
- Quality assurance regarding the fidelity of research-based instruction, strategies, and interventions
- The use of standard protocol interventions selected at Tiers 2 and 3

When a district is preparing to implement RtI as part of its LD identification process, the campus staff must clearly understand whose responsibility it is to collect and document assessment at each tier. Tier 1 assessment using universal screening is the responsibility of the general education classroom teacher for all students. However, it is also the responsibility of special education staff, educational diagnosticians, and school psychologists to consult with the general

individualized education plan (IEP) Either the educational program to be provided to a child with a disability or the written document that describes that program. Public schools are required by IDEA to develop an IEP for every student with a disability who meets the federal and state requirements for special education.

learning disability (LD) As defined by IDEA, "a disorder in one or more of the basic psychological processes involved in understanding or in using language, spoken or written, that may manifest itself in an imperfect ability to listen, think, speak, read, write, spell, or do mathematical calculations, including conditions such as perceptual disabilities, brain injury, minimal brain dysfunction, dyslexia, and developmental aphasia." Learning disabilities do *not* include "learning problems that are primarily the result of visual, hearing, or motor disabilities, of mental retardation, of emotional disturbance, or of environmental, cultural, or economic disadvantage" (34 CFR 300.8).

education staff on reviewing and interpreting the universal screening data.

Verifying and documenting the quality of the general education instruction and strategies are done by classroom teachers, support personnel, and the RtI team. The campus administrator is responsible for overseeing issues relating to fidelity and for providing support and resources as needed.

Progress monitoring—both academic and behavioral—is carried out by teachers, trained personnel, and members of the RtI team. The resulting data are interpreted by special educators, educational diagnosticians, and school psychologists.

The RtI team is responsible for problem solving to select Tier 2 and 3 interventions that are based on research and outlined in the district's guidelines for RtI and LD identification. The team is also responsible for documenting interventions and the fidelity of their delivery.

The assessment for special education is completed by trained and certified staff, such as educational diagnosticians, speech and language pathologists, and school psychologists. Because the RtI process continuously assesses student progress and needs, it contributes the data necessary for the special education eligibility assessment.

All districts are required to conform with state and federal regulations regarding eligibility determination under the IDEA 2004 mandate. According to federal standards, eligibility criteria should include information that identifies effective interventions. The data must be generated from multiple sources, and a variety of assessment methods must be used. Assessment must also take into consideration cultural, socioeconomic, racial, family history, language, and educational variables.

IEP team   The group of people responsible for developing, reviewing, and revising an individualized education plan.

Eligibility for special education continues to be decided by a team of professionals and parents (the IEP team). Team members include a representative of the local education agency (or LEA—generally the school district), parents, the general education teacher, a special education teacher, assessment personnel who can interpret the instructional implications of the assessment results, and others who have appropriate knowledge regarding the student and/or the disability condition. The data for the team's decision making include information that was collected during the RtI process, as well as the results of the special education full and individual evaluation.

full and individual evaluation
A comprehensive set of data gathered from multiple sources for each student being considered for special education and related services.

Within the federal requirements for special education eligibility, as specified by IDEA, are factors that are considered "exclusionary" to eligibility. A student will not be judged eligible for special education if one of these factors is identified as the primary reason for lack of progress:

- Lack of appropriate instruction in reading or math
- Limited English proficiency
- Cultural or economic disadvantage

In order for a student to be eligible for special education, the data collected must establish both the presence of a disability and the need for special education support or related services.

Educational progress is the focus of RtI, and progress data that are objective and linked to the intervention are essential. Progress-monitoring data that are important to determining eligibility include baseline data collected before the intervention; measurable goals derived from the baseline data; the learning rate, as documented on the intervention plan developed by the RtI team; and evaluation of the progress-monitoring data. The progress-monitoring data should include a comparison of the expected performance (outcome goal) and the measured performance (learning rate plotted on a CBM chart) during the intervention period. (For details, see "Monitoring Academic Progress with Curriculum-Based Measurement" in Chapter 4.)

The next question to ask is whether there is a difference between the student's performance and that of typical peers or expected standards (learning-rate difference). This issue is very complex and is defined according to state standards. IDEA 2004 allows states to *prohibit* the traditional approach of using a severe discrepancy between intelligence and achievement scores as the sole criterion for identifying a learning disability. The regulation also specifies that states *cannot require* the use of intelligence and achievement score discrepancy for determining learning disabilities. Also according to IDEA 2004, states are *required to permit* the use of a process (RtI) to determine whether a student responds to research-based intervention.

According to the National Association of State Directors of Special Education (NASDSE 2005), eligibility for special education is determined by integrating data collected from multiple sources that document the level of difference between the student's performance and that of peers. These sources include benchmark data (universal screening), learning-rate differences based on improvements (progress monitoring data, as charted against an aimline), documentation of a need for special education (how the student's learning is negatively affected by the skill deficit), and ruling out the exclusionary factors listed above.

All students are afforded protections under the IDEA 2004 requirements for assessment, procedural safeguards, and due process. Parents have the right to be informed, and their permission for assessing a student's special education eligibility must be obtained. Two aspects of this process should be addressed in relation to RtI: requests from parents to have their children assessed for special education eligibility; and independent evaluations of student eligibility for special education.

learning difference A difference between the student's performance and that of typical peers or expected standards.

independent educational evaluation As defined by IDEA, "an evaluation conducted by a qualified examiner who is not employed by the public agency responsible for the education of the child in question" (34 CFR 300.502).

Parental Request for Evaluation

Parents have the right to refer their child for testing for a suspected disability. This request may present a problem if prior documentation is not available regarding the student's exposure to research-based instruction, interventions used, and progress charting to identify whether a learning-rate difference exists. It is suggested that when a parent makes a request, the RtI team should review the request and the student's records. The team then examines the student's current instructional levels and assessment data (from universal screening, benchmarks, and classroom products). If it determines that the student has an educational need, the team may elect to start Tier 2 interventions and progress monitoring, or it may determine the need for Tier 3 interventions and assessment. If the progress-monitoring data are not available when the parent makes the request, the data must be collected. Communication between the RtI team and the parents is essential. If the parents believe that the only way their child can be successful is by categorizing or labeling the child, then the team has not done its job in explaining the RtI process. Parents need to be assured that the label does not drive the intervention and that their child will receive the necessary supports, regardless of a classification. It is vital that both staff and parents understand that identification of a learning disability needs to include progress-monitoring data that has been collected and reviewed.

Keep in mind that when a parent requests an evaluation of the child's eligibility for special education, the school district must either conduct the evaluation or give the parent written notice of its refusal to do so. A parent may request an evaluation prematurely, when Tier 1 and/or Tier 2 interventions have not yet been tried. In such a case, written notice of refusal is appropriate, but it must be done properly, in compliance with the law and regulations.

Independent Educational Evaluations

A parent has the right to request an independent educational evaluation (IEE) if the parent disagrees with the evaluation conducted by the school. The IEE process begins when a parent requests, in writing, an assessment that is conducted by an independent agent. A difficulty arises if the independent agent does not consider or have access to the RtI data: universal screening, interventions, and progress monitoring. It is essential that the district provide this information to the independent agent for consideration. The district should have a process in place that makes the data available to the independent agent. It is the responsibility of the independent agent to use and interpret the data appropriately in the context of the evaluation, and this may be problematic if the agent is not familiar with how to analyze the data in a meaningful way. The IEP team must consider the extent to which the independent agent used and interpreted the data to generate his or her conclusions and recommendations.

Lessons Learned: One campus conducted the RtI process and determined that a particular student was not eligible for special education, based on two factors: the learning-rate difference was not significant when the student's progress-monitoring graph was analyzed (that is, the student demonstrated some progress with intervention); and multiple measures used in the standardized assessment yielded average or low average scores, which did not indicate that the student was demonstrating a learning disability. Additionally, campus personnel had documented excessive tardies for the student. Campus staff were concerned that the student had not been afforded access to instruction, because of absences and the excessive tardies. An intervention plan was recommended to increase the student's attendance and access to the reading instruction, with extra tutorials and interventions. Progress-monitoring data revealed that when the student was present in class, his learning rates increased. Based on the data, the team decided that Tier 2 interventions were appropriate and that special education eligibility had not been established.

The parent disagreed with the team's decisions and requested an independent educational evaluation. The team gave the independent psychologist all relevant data pertaining to the student, and the psychologist's assessment results were consistent with those from the district's assessments. However, the psychologist did not use the progress-monitoring data or the school records of tardies as part of her evaluation, and she concluded that the student was indeed eligible for special education services because he was not passing his classes.

The campus IEP team invited the psychologist to the IEP meeting to go over the evaluation results. After much discussion, the psychologist admitted that the current intervention plan proposed by the team was appropriate and the student's eligibility for special education had not been established. The psychologist commented that she needed to "take some classes" to help her understand the RtI process and not immediately shift to a "categorizing mentality" when evaluating the needs of struggling students.

Reevaluation

Many questions have been asked about how reevaluations are conducted for students already identified as having a learning disability. Progress monitoring during Tiers 2 and 3 should continue and should be documented on the IEPs. The objective and goals of the IEPs should flow from the interventions and assessments that are part of the RtI process. Therefore reevaluation data can be derived from the progress monitoring and the documentation of learning rates. If a student who is receiving special education demonstrates progress on learning rates, the IEP team determines whether the student is ready to exit special education and move into less intensive support or should remain in special education. The critical determination is to establish whether the student continues to need special education services.

Epilogue

In the course of my consulting and training on RtI in numerous school districts, I have witnessed amazing results for both students and staff. I have seen staff who were reluctant or resistant to change become enthusiastic as they experienced self-growth and student progress. I have witnessed campuses transform the way they provide support services, and I have seen them achieve incredible results, ranging from increased student learning and motivation to the building of a cohesive staff.

As you walk down the path of Response to Intervention, take baby steps. Understand that you will make some mistakes and will reevaluate and revise your plans often. Remember: anything is possible with a positive attitude toward change. You can make the ordinary become extraordinary and, in the process, positively change the lives of children.

Appendix A
Frequently Asked Questions

Some common questions often come up when I consult on the Response to Intervention process. Here are the ones that seem to be foremost on the minds of most educators.

What is Response to Intervention?

Response to Intervention is practicing high-quality instruction and interventions that are matched to student needs. Ongoing assessment is used to monitor student progress on a frequent basis and to make important educational decisions.

Is this just another referral process defined by special education law?

No. Actually RtI was born out of the No Child Left Behind Act of 2001, which moved to improve accountability within the schools in order to promote adequate yearly progress for all children. The IDEA 2004 provisions of new guidelines for identification of learning disabilities aligned federal special education expectations to the No Child Left Behind Act, specifically with regard to the importance of a Response to Intervention model as part of the eligibility decision making.

What is the multi-tier model?

The multi-tier model is represented by a three- or four-tier paradigm. Tier 1 represents approximately 80 percent of all students, with all curriculum, instruction, and supports provided within the general education setting. In Tier 1 the most common assessments are universal screening and curriculum-based assessments. For those students (approximately 20 percent) who do not respond to Tier 1 curriculum, instruction, and supports, a team will provide Tier 2 interventions. In Tier 2, students receive individualized, intensive, research-based interventions in addition to Tier 1 supports and are assessed frequently using curriculum-based measurements. The students are monitored for a predetermined amount of time (9 to 12 weeks). Approximately 5 percent of students will show continued difficulty and a lack of progress, even with Tier 2 interventions. These students will then be provided Tier 3 interventions along with Tier 1 interventions. Tier 3 is simply an increase in the intensity of intervention and the frequency of curriculum-based measurements.

If a student moves to Tier 3, does that trigger an automatic referral for special education services?

No. In fact, entry into Tier 3 is a continuation of data collection to determine if the increased intervention may jump-start learning. Data collected during the first 6 to 8 weeks of Tier 3 can help the RtI team determine whether the student demonstrates progress or whether the student may need a comprehensive assessment to determine special education eligibility.

Who is responsible for making the decision of how RtI will work in my district?

Ideally I suggest that the district-level administrators (such as superintendent, curriculum coordinators, and special education administrators) work together to develop district guidelines. Once the guidelines are established, RtI then becomes a campus-based responsibility, with the campus administrator as the leader. The campus RtI team will be responsible for the RtI assessment, instruction, and intervention process.

What would be a good cutoff score for universal screening?

Ultimately the best way to determine a meaningful cutoff score is to develop local norms derived from curriculum-based assessments, but that takes time. A good guideline for this important decision point as a district begins assessments according to RtI would be to identify struggling learners as those students who fall below the 10th percentile on the instrument chosen for universal screening. One thing to consider is that the district may need to adjust the cutoff score after the first year's universal screening data have been gathered.

You have mentioned the importance of progress monitoring in this process. I understand the concept, but I want to know who will be responsible for administering the assessment.

The campus RtI team will determine the appropriate person(s) to carry out the progress monitoring. In Tier 1 all assessment is considered the responsibility of the general education teacher. In Tiers 2 and 3 the assessments may be completed by a standing member of the team, the person responsible for the interventions, or a designated staff member trained in administering, scoring, and documenting the assessment.

My principal asked me to be on the team, I am hesitant because I fear this is just one more thing for me to do. Will this be too much for me to handle with all my other extra responsibilities?

Team membership should be considered an honor. Team members should be respected for the amount of responsibility it takes to participate in and be an active member of the team. If you ever feel that this is an added burden, then your campus is not doing RtI right. It is recommended that the campus principal recognize the additional time and effort needed to be a team member, and honor that commitment by shifting the team member's current responsibilities to other staff.

What happens when a parent requests testing or when we get a prescription form requesting a test by a doctor?

All requests must be reviewed by the team. It is important to note that such requests do not automatically fast-forward the assessment to a comprehensive evaluation. The team has a responsibility to review all data and use the data in a consistent manner to make decisions. If there are data indicating that the child is struggling, the team needs to decide the level of intervention, develop specific interventions, and determine appropriate assessments. Remember that a parent request for an evaluation triggers a legal responsibility. The district must either conduct the evaluation or give a proper written notice of its refusal to do so. So if the team concludes that an evaluation is not called for, the team should be sure to provide the written notice of refusal in the manner required by regulations.

Do you have a list of research-based interventions we should use?

The No Child Left Behind Act specifies criteria for meeting its "scientifically based research" standards. Although there is not an exhaustive list, there are interventions that have met the standard. Interventions regarding delivery of instruction range from cooperative grouping and accommodation of learning styles to peer-assisted tutoring and differentiated instruction techniques. Specific intervention strategies that are more intense and individualized have been investigated by the What Works Clearinghouse (ies.ed.gov/ncee/wwc), which is sponsored by the U.S. Department of Education. There are also other interventions listed in this book that may aid you in the search. I recommend that the district first inventory all interventions already in place and review the literature to determine if those interventions meet research-based standards.

Appendix B

Sample Forms from the Willis (Texas) Independent School District

---

Willis Independent School District   Behavior and Education Support for Teachers (BEST)

Meeting Minutes

Meeting # _____   Date _____

Minutes

_____

_____

_____

_____

_____

_____

_____

_____

_____

_____

_____

_____

_____

_____

_____

_____

_____

_____

_____

BEST Committee Members

Signature   Position

_____

_____

_____

_____

_____

_____

_____

Willis Independent School District   Behavior and Education Support for Teachers (BEST)

Student Data Documentation Form

Student _____   Teacher _____

Campus _____   Grade _____ DOB_____

☐ Hearing/vision screening

☐ BEST Information Packet

☐ Learning and Behavior Problem Checklist

☐ Copy of registration card

☐ Report card and/or progress report

☐ Student work samples (journal, spelling tests, math computation)

☐ Information from Parents form

☐ Copy of literacy folder grid sheet (yellow folder)

For office use only

BEST Team Meeting Dates:

_____ _____ _____ _____ _____

Willis Independent School District   Behavior and Education Support for Teachers (BEST)

Student Referral Form

Teacher(s)_____   Date Received _____

Student Name _____   Grade_____   DOB _____

*Parent Contact Date _____   ☐ Conference   ☐ Telephone   ☐ Note   ☐ E-mail

*Second Contact Date_____   ☐ Conference   ☐ Telephone   ☐ Note   ☐ E-mail

Reason for Referral: ☐ Academic   ☐ Absences (# ___)   ☐ Tardies (# ___)   ☐ Behavioral   ☐ Office Referrals (# ___)

Free/Reduced: ☐ Yes   ☐ No

Testing (Check those that are current.)

       ☐ TPRI   Score: _____

       ☐ ITBS   Score(s): Reading _____   Math _____

       ☐ KBIT   Score(s): Vocabulary _____   Matrices _____

       ☐ Rigby   _____   _____   _____

       ☐ COGAT   _____   _____   _____

       ☐ TAKS

Grade	Reading	Math	Writing

*Current TAKS Benchmark Scores: Reading _____   Math _____   Writing _____

Prior Special Ed Referral   ☐ Yes   ☐ No

Prior Retention   ☐ Yes   ☐ No   Grade _____

Subject(s) Currently Failing   _____

Prior Districts   ☐ Yes   ☐ No   # of Districts _____

Services Provided

    ☐ Speech   ☐ Literacy Lab   ☐ Dyslexia   ☐ AIM

    ☐ Mentoring   ☐ Learning Centers   ☐ Resource   ☐ START-IN

    ☐ Tutorials_____   ☐ Plato   ☐ Bilingual/ESL   ☐ Content Mastery/Learning Lab/STAR

    ☐ Waterford_____   ☐ Sleek   ☐ Counseling   ☐ Other _____

(* Mandatory prior to meeting)   Page 1 of 3

Willis Independent School District   Student Referral Form (continued)

Please describe the **specific concerns** prompting this referral. What makes this student difficult to teach? List any academic, social, emotional, or medical factors that negatively impact the student's performance.

_____

_____

_____

_____

How do this student's academic skills compare with those of an average student in your classroom?

_____

_____

_____

In what settings/situations does the problem occur **most** often?

_____

In what settings/situations does the problem occur **least** often?

_____

What are the student's strengths, talents, and/or specific interests?

1. _____

2. _____

3. _____

What would be the best day(s) and time(s) for someone to observe the student having the difficulties that you describe above? (Please attach a copy of the student's daily schedule, if available.)

_____

Please provide any additional pertinent information such as this student's most current report card, schedule, and attendance record, and return them with referral.

Willis Independent School District   Student Referral Form (continued)

Allowable Accommodations

	Intervention	(Circle one)				How Often		
		Successful (S)	Unsuccessful (US)	Not Tried (NT	Not Applicable (NA)	Daily	Weekly	Monthly
1	Teacher-led one-on-one	S	US	NT	NA			
2	Teacher-led small groups	S	US	NT	NA			
3	Change seating	S	US	NT	NA			
4	Reduce distractions	S	US	NT	NA			
5	Provide breaks	S	US	NT	NA			
6	Use visual cues/signals	S	US	NT	NA			
7	Modify instructions	S	US	NT	NA			
8	Tutor/Mentor (☐ peer ☐ volunteer)	S	US	NT	NA			
9	Reduce degree of difficulty	S	US	NT	NA			
10	Allow more time	S	US	NT	NA			
11	Give immediate feedback	S	US	NT	NA			
12	Maintain proximity	S	US	NT	NA			
13	Use timer	S	US	NT	NA			
14	Break task into smaller steps	S	US	NT	NA			
15	Minimize transition time	S	US	NT	NA			
16	Model/role-play behavior	S	US	NT	NA			
17	Individual instruction/attention	S	US	NT	NA			
18	Positive reinforcement	S	US	NT	NA			
	☐ verbal ☐ concrete	S	US	NT	NA			
19	Planned ignoring	S	US	NT	NA			
20	Contract/chart/points	S	US	NT	NA			
	☐ classroom ☐ CM	S	US	NT	NA			
21	Loss of privileges	S	US	NT	NA			
22	Privileges/responsibilities	S	US	NT	NA			
23	Time-out (in room)	S	US	NT	NA			
24	Time-out (out of room)	S	US	NT	NA			

What activities or strategies have you tried to do to resolve this problem?

_____

_____

_____

Willis Independent School District   Behavior and Education Support for Teachers (BEST)

BEST Meeting Checklist

Please bring these items to your scheduled BEST meeting:

- ☐ Cumulative folder
- ☐ Most current progress report/report card
- ☐ Monitoring folder (orange folder with brads)
- ☐ Rigby protocol
- ☐ Compass report (TPRI)

Student _____

Meeting date_____

- -

Willis Independent School District   Behavior and Education Support for Teachers (BEST)

BEST Meeting Checklist

Please bring these items to your scheduled BEST meeting:

- ☐ Cumulative folder
- ☐ Most current progress report/report card
- ☐ Monitoring folder (orange folder with brads)
- ☐ Rigby protocol
- ☐ Compass report (TPRI)

Student _____

Meeting date_____

Willis Independent School District

Behavior and Education Support for Teachers (BEST)

Student Progress-Monitoring Form

Student _____

Skill Area _____

Measured By _____

Intervention	Activity	Results from Data Collection/Analysis				
		Date		Date		Date

Willis Independent School District   Behavior and Education Support for Teachers (BEST)

Information from Parents

Name _____ SSN_____ Medicaid # _____

School_____ Grade _____ DOB_____

Address _____ Phone# _____ Emergency # _____

Parents were contacted by   ☐ Letter   ☐ Telephone   ☐ Conference

Parents were contacted by _____ on_____

(School staff)   (Date)

Family

| With whom does the student live? | |
| Who has legal authority to make educational decisions for this child? | |

Primary language spoken in the home _____Other languages spoken _____

Father's name	Age	Occupation	Mother's name	Age	Occupation
Father's employer	Work phone number		Mother's employer	Work phone number	
Father's highest grade completed:			Mother's highest grade completed:		
Father's learning, attention, behavior, or medical problems? If so, please specify.			Mother's learning, attention, behavior, or medical problems? If so, please specify.		

Other children in the home	Age	Relationship	Other adults in the home	Age	Relationship

Have any of your blood relatives experienced problems similar to those your child is experiencing?   ☐ Yes ☐ No
If yes, please describe:

_____

_____

_____

Willis Independent School District   Behavior and Education Support for Teachers (BEST)

Child Behaviors

What are some of your child's strengths?

_____

_____

_____

Do you feel that your child is experiencing problems in school? What kind of problems?

_____

_____

_____

When were you first aware of the problem?

_____

_____

_____

What do you think is causing the problem?

_____

_____

_____

Has your child mentioned problems with school? How does he/she feel about the problem?

_____

_____

_____

Please describe your child's behavior at home. (For example, is he/she generally well-behaved? Have there been any recent changes in behavior? How does he/she get along with other family members, neighbors, and friends?)

_____

_____

_____

What does your child do when not in school? (For example, watch TV, read, do chores, work at part-time job, play with other children.)

_____

_____

_____

What activities does the family do together? (For example, watch TV, go camping, participate in hobbies, sports.)

_____

_____

_____

Page 2 of 4

Willis Independent School District   Behavior and Education Support for Teachers (BEST)

What methods of discipline are used with your child at home? (For example, spanking, extra chores, early bedtime, removal of TV and other privileges, rewards for good behavior.)

_____

_____

_____

What is your child's reaction to discipline?

_____

_____

_____

Have there been any important changes within the family? (For example, parent job changes, moves, births, deaths, illnesses, accidents, separations, divorce, remarriage, abuse incidents.)

_____

_____

_____

Briefly discuss any other important information about your child.

_____

_____

_____

Health and Developmental History

Were there any problems before, during, or immediately after birth?   ☐ Yes   ☐ No
If yes, please explain.

_____

_____

_____

Compared with other children in the family, the child's development has been:
☐ slower   ☐ about the same   ☐ faster

Describe any problems during infancy or early childhood with feeding, sleeping, or other areas such as difficulty being comforted, excessive restlessness or irritability, colicky, etc.

_____

_____

Circle below the characteristics of your child 's temperament when he/she was an infant and a toddler.

Activity level	Low	Average	High
Attention level	Low	Average	High
Adaptability—Dealing with changes	Poor	Good	Very good
Approach/withdrawal—Responding to new things (e.g., places, people, food, etc.)	Poor	Good	Very good
Mood—What was your child's basic mood?	Unhappy	Average	Very happy
Regularity—How predictable was your child in patterns of sleep, appetite, etc.?	Not predictable	Somewhat predictable	Very predictable

Page 3 of 4

Willis Independent School District   Behavior and Education Support for Teachers (BEST)

Briefly describe any childhood illnesses (e.g., measles, chicken pox, chronic ear infections, allergies, high fevers, or seizures), accidents (e.g., head injury, broken bones, stitches), and hospitalizations. Please give your child's age at the time of illness, accident, or hospitalization.

_____

_____

_____

Is your child under the care of a physician for a medical problem? ☐ Yes   ☐ No   If yes, please explain.

_____

_____

_____

Please indicate the date and results of your child's latest physical examination.

_____

_____

_____

Is your child now taking medicine?   ☐ Yes   ☐ No   If yes, please describe reason for medication, type, dosage, and effect and side effects the medicine might have.

_____

_____

Has your child ever taken medicine for a long period of time? ☐ Yes   ☐ No   If yes, please explain the reasons and effect.

_____

_____

Does you child use any special equipment or technology to improve functioning?   ☐ Yes   ☐ No
If yes, please explain.

_____

_____

Is your child receiving services from another agency (e.g., tutoring, counseling, probation monitoring, etc.)?
☐ Yes   ☐ No   If yes, please explain.

_____

_____

Has your child ever been evaluated before for neurological, psychological, psychiatric, speech language, learning, hearing, vision, or physical problems in the past? ☐ Yes   ☐ No   If yes, please explain and indicate dates of assessments.

_____

_____

Would you be interested in parent training? ☐ Yes   ☐ No   If yes, in what areas?

_____

_____

_____   _____
               Signature   Date

Appendix C
Online Resources

This is a list of online resources I have found most helpful when consulting with school district staff about Response to Intervention. Although this list is by no means exhaustive, it includes the resources necessary for developing and implementing a Response to Intervention model.

Leadership Characteristics for Administrators Who Are Facilitating Change

Center for Educational Networking: www.cenmi.org

Southwest Educational Development Laboratory (SEDL):
   www.sedl.org/change/leadership/intro.html

Assessment

AIMSweb: www.aimsweb.com

Dynamic Indicators of Basic Early Literacy Skills (DIBELS): dibels.uoregon.edu

Intervention Central (CBM Warehouse): www.interventioncentral.org

National Center on Student Progress Monitoring: www.studentprogress.org

Screening to Enhance Educational Performance (STEEP): www.isteep.com

Texas Primary Reading Inventory: www.tpri.org

Academic Interventions and Instructional Strategies

The Access Center: Improving Outcomes for All Students K–8: www
   .k8accesscenter.org

Cooperative Learning: edtech.kennesaw.edu/intech/cooperativelearning.htm

Corrective Reading: www.sraonline.com

The Florida Center for Reading Research: www.fcrr.org

Intervention Central: www.interventioncentral.org

Learning Styles: www.learningstyles.net

Peer-Assisted Learning Strategies (PALS): kc.vanderbilt.edu/pals/

Promising Practices Network: www.promisingpractices.net

Strategies for Differentiating Instruction: members.shaw.ca/
   priscillatheroux/differentiatingstrategies.html

Vaughn Gross Center for Reading and Language Arts:
  www.texasreading.org/utcrla/
What Works Clearinghouse: www.whatworks.ed.gov

Behavior Strategies and Interventions

CBM Warehouse: www.interventioncentral.org
Character Counts! www.charactercounts.org
Character Education Organizations and Initiatives: www.cortland.edu/
  character/chared_orgs.html
National Association of School Psychologists: www.nasponline.org
Positive Behavioral Interventions and Supports: www.pbis.org
Project Achieve: www.projectachieve.info
Project Resilience: www.projectresilience.com
Rhode Island Technical Assistance Project: www.ritap.org
Social Skills Resources: uscm.med.sc.edu/CDR/social%20skills.html

RtI Process

National Association of State Directors of Special Education: www.nasdse.org
Office of Special Education and Rehabilitative Services: www
  .osepideasthatwork/toolkit/ta_responsiveness_intervention.asp

Parents

LD OnLine: www.ldonline.org
Response to Intervention (RTI): A Primer for Parents: www.ldonline.org/
  article/15857 or nasponline.org/resources/handouts/rtiprimer.pdf

Glossary

Abbreviations

CBM curriculum-based measurement

ESL English as a second language

IDEA Individuals with Disabilities Education Improvement Act of 2004

IEE independent educational evaluation

IEP individualized education plan

LD learning disability

LEA local education agency

NASDSE National Association of State Directors of Special Education

NCLB No Child Left Behind Act

RtI Response to Intervention

Terms

across-condition control design An experimental technique in which different conditions are measured using the same subjects.

aimline A visual representation (line) on a progress monitoring graph that connects the baseline data point to the outcome goal.

align To reorganize and modify components as needed so that they form a unified system.

antecedent event An event that triggers a problem behavior.

assessment The process of using evaluation tools to gather and analyze information about student skill level and progress and the effectiveness of curricula and teaching methods.

baseline data point An initial score that indicates a student's skill level before intervention; serves as the starting point in curriculum-based measurement of the student's response to the intervention.

consequence What happens immediately after a behavior occurs.

criterion-referenced assessment A measure of performance in terms of a clearly defined learning task.

curricular variable A quantifiable event or circumstance related to the instruction of students in the schools.

curriculum The set of courses, coursework, and content offered at a school.

curriculum-based measurement (CBM) Any set of assessment procedures that use direct observation and recording of a student's performance in a local curriculum to gather information for making instructional decisions.

cutoff score Within RtI, a preset score set to help identify struggling learners during universal screening at Tier 1.

data-point decision rule A means of interpreting curriculum-based measurement data (points on a graph) in order to make decisions about a student's intervention plan.

decision points Guidelines developed by the district for gauging whether a student may need more intensive interventions within the RtI process.

delivery of instruction The methods for introducing information to students.

developmental skill progression The process of acquiring the basic skills necessary for learning to occur.

diagnostics A precise form of assessment that analyzes individual student strengths and weaknesses.

differentiated instruction An approach to teaching and learning in which students have multiple options for taking in information and making sense of ideas; requires teachers to be flexible in adjusting their methods and the curriculum to suit students, rather than expecting students to modify themselves for the curriculum.

direct observations Systematic, structured observations that use well-designed observation record forms.

disordered thoughts Abnormal thoughts associated with emotional conditions.

documentation Any material (such as student products, tests, written reports) containing data gathered during the RtI process.

educational diagnostician A professional with an ability to assess and diagnose the learning problems of students.

eligibility conditions Conditions defined by federal and state governments for determining whether children qualify to receive special education services.

emotional disturbance eligibility Qualification of a student as eligible to receive special supports to counteract a chronic behavior or emotional condition that adversely affects his or her educational performance.

environmental triggers Events or situations in the student's environment that bring about a behavioral response.

fidelity The degree to which something is carried out as designed, intended, or planned.

fluency An acceptable level of mastery of a skill.

full and individual evaluation A comprehensive set of data gathered from multiple sources for each student being considered for special education and related services.

functional behavioral assessment A collection of information about events that predict and maintain a student's problem behavior; used to construct a behavior action plan.

functional communication The use of language in a meaningful and understandable way.

hypothesis statement In the functional behavioral assessment, the statement that identifies the function that maintains a student's problem behavior (what the student gets out of the behavior).

IEP team The group of people responsible for developing, reviewing, and revising an individualized education plan.

independent educational evaluation (IEE) As defined by IDEA, "an evaluation conducted by a qualified examiner who is not employed by the public agency responsible for the education of the child in question" (34 CFR 300.502).

individualized education plan (IEP) Either the educational program to be provided to a child with a disability or the written document that describes that program. Public schools are required by IDEA to develop an IEP for every student with a disability who meets the federal and state requirements for special education.

instruction The act of delivering information so that learning can occur.

instructional effectiveness A measure of a teacher's delivery of instruction, based on the positive learning outcomes of students.

instructional variable A quantifiable event or circumstance related to the action, practice, or profession of teaching.

intervention Any process that has the effect of increasing learning or modifying a student's behavior.

interventionists Persons trained in specific aspects of academic and behavioral interventions.

intrinsic motivation Motivation that is governed by an individual's internal drives.

learning disability As defined by IDEA, "a disorder in one or more of the basic psychological processes involved in understanding or in using language, spoken or written, that may manifest itself in an imperfect ability to listen, think, speak, read, write, spell, or do mathematical calculations, including conditions such as perceptual disabilities, brain injury, minimal brain dysfunction, dyslexia, and developmental aphasia." Learning disabilities do *not* include "learning problems that are primarily the result of visual, hearing, or motor disabilities, of mental retardation, of emotional disturbance, or of environmental, cultural, or economic disadvantage" (34 CFR 300.8).

learning rate The pace of a student's skill acquisition; one of the elements used for making decisions in RtI.

learning style The method of learning, individualized to a student, that allows the student to learn most easily and effectively.

norm-referenced assessment A measure of performance in terms of an individual's standing in some known group, such as all of a district's students at a particular grade level.

operational definition A description of behaviors that are observable and measurable.

outcome goal The targeted goal of an intervention plan.

paraeducators Support members of the learning and teaching team who ensure that students receive multiple levels of support in schools.

passive noncompliance The failure of a student to perform a teacher's request, often by acting as if he or she did not hear it.

peer-assisted learning A specific research-based intervention that uses class-wide peer tutoring techniques developed by Doug and Lynn Fuchs.

performance Measurable outcomes that are characteristic of student learning.

performance deficit An inability to demonstrate a skill that has been learned.

phoneme segmentation The ability to break up and identify the sounds within words.

phonemic awareness Awareness of the sounds of language and how they make up words and sentences.

phonics An instructional design that involves teaching children to read by connecting sounds with letters or groups of letters.

Plato Learning lab An intervention designed to increase learning and teaching effectiveness by addressing the entire spectrum of academic needs within a classroom.

positive behavior support system A systematic approach that clearly establishes behavioral expectations and uses reinforcement when the student demonstrates appropriate behaviors.

positive reinforcement The process of associating a desired behavior with a desired consequence, which then increases the probability that the behavior will be repeated.

pre-referral assessment An evaluation of whether further assessment is needed to determine a student's special education eligibility. This type of assessment does not focus on developing intervention strategies.

pre-referral team A campus-level team of teachers, counselors, administrators, and support personnel that meets on a regular basis to discuss students who are demonstrating difficulty in the general education setting.

preventive Refers to action (such as early intervention) undertaken to avoid failure.

proactive Refers to action that anticipates future needs or problems, such as putting supports in place to increase the probability of successful learning outcomes and positive behaviors in the classroom.

probes In terms of progress monitoring and curriculum-based measurement, refers to brief repeated assessments of an academic skill.

problem behavior Behavior that has been identified as impeding the learning of the student or of others in the student's environment.

problem-solving method A set of specific steps for solving problems related to the challenging aspects of teaching and learning.

progress monitoring Frequent measurement of student progress in a brief, repeatable, reliable, and scientifically valid way; usually performed at predetermined intervals to allow for timely modification of instructional design to suit the student's needs.

prosocial behaviors Actions that are intended to benefit others in social situations.

random-assignment experimental design An experimental technique in which subjects randomly receive different treatments (or no treatment).

Reading First initiative A process whereby states and districts receive support from the federal government for applying scientifically based research to ensure that all children learn to read well by the end of third grade.

referral-to-test model A service delivery model in which a student must be referred to a campus team and tested for eligibility before receiving special education supports and services.

research-based strategies Instructional designs and recommendations that have been demonstrated through formal scientific research to improve learning.

retention rate A measure of a student's ability to retain and demonstrate a previously learned skill.

RtI model A conception of the process known as Response to Intervention for delivering scientifically based instruction and interventions to facilitate student learning.

school organization system The administrative, functional, and personnel structure of a school system.

screening A type of assessment used to predict which students are likely to experience difficulty learning.

Section 504 committee A school-based team that meets to discuss the needs of a student with a disability condition and how the condition affects learning. (Section 504 is a federal law that prohibits discrimination against individuals with disabilities.)

service delivery model A description of the way in which services—such as classroom placement, strategic interventions, peer tutoring, cooperative grouping, and differentiated instruction—will be provided to students.

setting event An event that is removed in time from the occurrence of a problem behavior but is related to it.

skill deficit A deficiency in a skill that is necessary for learning to occur or for achieving competence in a given area.

sound blending The blending of sounds together to form words.

staff development Intensive and ongoing training for teachers, administrators, and educational specialists, with a goal of improving the performance of both staff and students.

standardized assessment A type of test that is developed according to standard procedures and is administered and scored in a consistent manner for all students.

standard protocol Interventions that match a set of research-based practices to students who show predictable patterns of performance.

structural variables Quantifiable events or circumstances related to a school system's pattern of organization.

structured observation technique A formal method of observing students and the environment.

struggling learners Students with characteristics that indicate they have a higher chance of failing in the areas of learning and behavior.

student product Something created by a student to demonstrate learning of a skill.

student-based interventions Interventions specifically designed for individual students.

tiers of intervention Levels of increasingly intense interventions to help students learn.

universal strategies Instructional and behavioral strategies that are available to all students.

validity The degree to which a test measures what it was designed to measure.

within-condition experimental design An experimental technique in which the same subjects are tested on a single condition.

within-student issue An issue that is due to a student's learning abilities.

Bibliography

Batsche, G., J. Elliott, J. L. Graden, J. Grimes, J. F. Kovaleski, D. Prasse, D. J. Reschly, J. Schrag, and W. D. Tilly III. 2005. *Response to Intervention: Policy considerations and implementation*. Alexandria, VA: National Association of State Directors of Special Education.

Berninger, V., and S. Abbott. 2003. *PAL research-supported reading and writing lessons*. San Antonio, TX: Psychological Corporation.

Deno, S. L. 1987. Curriculum-based measurement: An introduction. *Teaching Exceptional Children* 20: 41–44.

Deno, S. L., A. Reschly-Anderson, E. Lembke, H. Zorka, and S. Callender. 2002. A model for schoolwide implementation: A case example. Paper presented at the National Association of School Psychologists, Chicago.

Englemann, S., and D. Carmine. 1982. *A theory of instruction, principles, and applications*. New York: Irvington.

Fisher, Douglas. 2000. Curriculum and instruction for all abilities and intelligences. *High School Magazine* 7(7): 21–25.

Fuchs, D., and L. S. Fuchs. 2005. Responsiveness-to-intervention: A blueprint for practitioners, policymakers, and parents. *Teaching Exceptional Children* 38(1): 57–61.

Fuchs, D., L. Fuchs, J. Hintz, and E. Lenke. 2006. Progress monitoring in the context of Responsiveness to Intervention. Paper presented at the National Center on Student Progress Monitoring Summer Institute, Kansas City, MO.

Good, R. H., J. Gruba, and R. A. Kaminski. 2001. Best practices in using Dynamic Indicators of Basic Early Literacy Skills (DIBELS) in an outcomes-driven model. In A. Thomas and J. Grimes, eds., *Best practices in school psychology IV*, 697–700. Washington, DC: National Association of School Psychologists.

Gordon, C. 2002. *Methods for measuring the influence of concept mapping on student information literacy*. Chicago: American Library Association.

Individuals with Disabilities Education Improvement Act of 2004 (IDEA). PL 108-446. http://www.copyright.gov/legislation/pl108-446.pdf.

Jenson, W. R., H. K. Reavis, and G. Rhode. 1998. *The tough kid book*. Longmont, CO: Sopris West.

Jimerson, S. R., M. K. Burns, and A. M. VanDerHeyden. 2007. *Handbook of Response to Intervention: The science and practice of assessment and intervention*. New York: Springer.

Johnson, E., D. F. Mellard, D. Fuchs, and M. A. McKnight. 2006. *Responsiveness to Intervention (RtI): How to do it*. Lawrence, KS: National Research Center on Learning Disabilities.

Kaminski, R., and R. Good. 1998. Assessing early literacy skills in a problem solving model: Dynamic Indicators of Basic Early Literacy Skills. In M. R. Shinn, ed., *Advanced applications of curriculum-based measurement.* New York: Guilford.

Kilpatrick, J., J. Swafford, and J. Findell, eds. 2001. *Adding it up: Helping children learn mathematics,* by Mathematics Learning Study Committee. Washington, DC: National Academy Press.

Knoff, H. M., and G. M. Batsche. 1995. Project ACHIEVE: Analyzing a school reform process for at-risk and underachieving students. *School Psychology Review* 24:579–603.

Kovaleski, J. F., E. E. Gickling, and H. Morrow. 1999. High versus low implementation of instructional support teams: A case for maintaining program fidelity. *Remedial and Special Education* 20:170–183.

Maxwell, J.C. 2000. *Failing Forward: Turning mistakes into stepping stones for success.* Nashville, TN: Thomas Nelson.

McCook, John E. 2006. *The RtI guide: Developing and implementing a model in your schools.* Horsham, PA: LRP Publications.

McKenzie, Jamie. 2003. Inspired Investigations. *Educational Technology Journal* 12(5): 2003.

Méndez-Morse, S. 1992. *Leadership characteristics that facilitate school change.* Austin, TX: Southwest Regional Development Laboratory.

NASDSE. 2005. *Response to Intervention: Policy considerations and implementation.* Alexandria, VA: National Association of State Directors of Special Education.

National Joint Committee on Learning Disabilities. 2005. *Responsiveness to Intervention and Learning Disabilities.* http://www.ncld.org/index.php?option=content&task=view&id=591.

National Staff Development Council. 2001. *Standards for staff development.* Rev. ed. Oxford, OH.

No Child Left Behind Act of 2001 (NCLB). PL 107-110. http://www.ed.gov/policy/elsec/leg/esea02/107-110.pdf.

Ownby, R., F. Wallbrown, A. D'Atri, and B. Armstrong. 1985. Patterns of referrals for school psychological services: Replication of the referral problems category system. *Special Services in the School* 1(4): 53–66.

President's Commission on Excellence in Special Education. 2002. *A new era: Revitalizing special education for children and their families.* Washington, DC: U.S. Department of Education.

Reid, M. I., L. R. Clunies-Ross, B. Goacher, and C. Vile. 1981. Mixed ability teaching: Problems and possibilities. *Educational Research* 24(1): 3–10.

Sattler, J. M. 2002. *Assessment of children: Behavioral and clinical applications.* 4th ed. La Mesa, CA: Jerome M. Sattler.

Schniedewind, N., and E. Davidson. 2000. Differentiating cooperative learning. *Educational Leadership* 58(1): 24–27.

Shapiro, E. S. 1996. *Academic skills problems: Direct assessment and intervention.* New York: Guilford.

Shinn, M. 1989. *Curriculum–based measurement: Assessing special children.* New York: Guilford.

Showers, B., B. Joyce, and B. Bennett. 1987. Synthesis of research on staff development: A framework for future study and state of the art analysis. *Educational Leadership* 45(3): 77–87.

Sprick, R. 1998. *CHAMPs: A proactive and positive approach to classroom management.* Longmont, CO: Sopris West.

Tindal, G., J. Hasbrouck, and C. Jones. 2005. *Oral reading fluency: 90 years of measurement.* Eugene, OR: Behavioral Research and Teaching.

Tomlinson, C. A. 1995. Differentiating Instruction for Advanced Learners in the Mixed-Ability Middle School Classroom. *ERIC Digest* E536 (October). http://www.ericdigests.org/1996-3/mixed.htm.

Wright, J. 2006. CBM workshop manual. http://www.interventioncentral.org.

ANDREA OGONOSKY is an educational consultant residing in Humble, Texas. Andrea supervises licensed specialists in school psychology within the greater Houston area and provides consultative support to school districts around the state in the areas of learning disabilities, emotional disturbance, autism, ADHD, and Tourette's syndrome, in addition to supplying expert testimony at special education due-process hearings. She currently develops and provides trainings focusing on assessment, interventions, and system support of the Response to Intervention process in Texas and Arkansas. Andrea began her educational career in Pennsylvania and was actively involved with the beginning implementation of the Instructional Support Team process there. Upon relocating to Texas, she served as a district-level school psychologist and coordinator of psychological and diagnostic services in the Humble ISD, where she began a pilot program involving curriculum-based measurement. She also was employed at the Region 4 Education Service Center prior to her current practice as an educational consultant. Andrea holds a doctorate in school psychology from the Pennsylvania State University and is a past president of the Texas Association of School Psychologists. Please refer to Andrea's website *www.ogonoskyrti.com* for additional RTI information. She can be contacted at aogonosky@msn.com.